PENGUIN BOOKS

THE FRAGRANCE OF BASIL

Originally from Milan, Raffaela has lived in Auckland with her husband and two daughters for the past four years. Leaving behind stressful careers as chartered accountants, they moved to New Zealand to experience a complete change of lifestyle.

Raffaela grew up in a family where diverse regional influences resulted in a mixture of flavours and food cultures – a real *minestrone* of feelings and emotions. Her love of cooking soon passed from a simple interest in traditional dishes to savour in the company of friends, to researching and delving into the more technical, historical and cultural aspects of culinary art. This passion led to her spending several years attending courses at the Culinary Institute of Milan, and more recently to studying the innovative new recipes developed by the most famous Italian chefs.

In 1999 she established *Al Dente*, her own food consultancy, to promote both traditional Italian cuisine as well as new food trends as they evolve in Italy. www.aldente.co.nz

Cooking – her passion and her work – and even more so her nostalgia for particular aromas only found in Italy, lead her to spend large periods of time every year in search of places and traditions which remain hidden to most people.

Together with her husband, Paolo, they co-ordinate the Auckland Slow Food Chapter.

SIMONE SCHENIRER

Simone was born in Auckland to a French mother and Polish father. Her love affair with Italy, its language, culture and peoples, began at age sixteen and she has spent the last twenty-two years travelling between New Zealand and Italy to work, study and live.

Simone completed a BA in History and Italian in 1983, but was motivated by a desire to maintain her links with the language and culture while living in New Zealand by undertaking and completing an MA in Italian with first class honours in 1999. She spent time outside her second home in Florence (she has left shoes there) to research her thesis on the verbal and non-verbal language of the Sicilian Mafia in Palermo.

Translating Raffaela's story has been a technical and linguistic challenge for Simone as well as a great pleasure. While Simone encourages anyone with a genuine passion for things Italian to attempt to learn the language, she is delighted and honoured to have been given the opportunity of bringing Raffaela's story and talent to the attention of an English-speaking audience.

THE FRAGRANCE OF BASIL

Food & Memories of My Italian Childhood

Raffaela Delmonte

Translated by Simone Schenirer
Drawings by Mirella Santini

PENGUIN BOOKS

PENGUIN BOOKS
Penguin Books (NZ) Ltd, cnr Airborne and Rosedale Roads, Albany,
Auckland 1310, New Zealand
Penguin Books Ltd, 80 Strand, London, WC2R 0RL, England
Penguin Putnam Inc, 375 Hudson Street, New York, NY 10014, United States
Penguin Books Australia Ltd, 250 Camberwell Road, Camberwell,
Victoria 3124, Australia
Penguin Books Canada Ltd, 10 Alcorn Avenue, Toronto,
Ontario, Canada M4V 3B2
Penguin Books (South Africa) (Pty) Ltd, 24 Sturdee Avenue, Rosebank,
Johannesburg 2196, South Africa
Penguin Books India (P) Ltd, 11, Community Centre, Panchsheel Park,
New Delhi 110 017, India
Penguin Books Ltd, Registered Offices: Harmondsworth, Middlesex, England

First published by Penguin Books (NZ) Ltd, 2002

1 3 5 7 9 10 8 6 4 2

Copyright © text and photographs Raffaela Delmonte, 2002
Copyright © drawings Mirella Santini, 2002

The right of Raffaela Delmonte to be identified as the author of this work in
terms of section 96 of the Copyright Act 1994 is hereby asserted.

Editorial services by Michael Gifkins & Associates
Designed by Mary Egan
Typeset by Egan-Reid Ltd
Translated by Simone Schenirer
Printed in Australia by McPherson's Printing Group

ISBN 0 14 301829 9
www.penguin.co.nz

ACKNOWLEDGEMENTS

To Simone, who has been so much more than just a translator, but also a friend and companion in both the enthusiasm and doubts that have accompanied the writing of this book. For the English edition, I consider Simone my co-author.

To Nadia Ganassin, unparalleled translator of recipes and generous culinary advisor.

To my mother, Mirella, for the beautiful sketches that embellish the text, drawn with maternal love and seasoned with a dash of genius and eccentricity.

To my sister Giudi, who has encouraged me from afar, and with great patience supported my whims and flights of fancy.

To my wonderful family, to all my relatives and friends who have showered me with the love and warmth that I hope will warm the hearts of all who read this book.

AUTHOR'S NOTE

The recipes in this book serve four people, unless otherwise stated, taking into consideration that they form part of a menu normally composed of more than one dish as is customary with Italian eating habits. Cooking temperatures and times are a guide only. The most commonly used flour in Italian baking is Tipo '00'. Sometimes I indicate a possible substitute.

Because the language of Italy is so intimately linked with its food, Italian terms are used throughout and are translated only as necessary, either in the text or as a footnote. Further translations and more detailed explanations are arranged in the glossary at the end of each chapter. These can be read for interest quite separately from the text.

Note: 1 glass is 140–150 ml

LIST OF RECIPES

CONTENTS

*A mia mamma Mirella e alla mia
sorellona Giudi nel ricordo di papa' Nini.*

La mente dell'uomo pensa molto alla sua via,
ma e' il Signore che dirige i suoi passi.

PROVERBS, CH. 15, V. 9

FOREWORD

In her first paragraph Raffaela tells us everything we need to know about her.

'Cooking . . . is the subtle thread which unites my diverse family, as well as the only proven method of communicating the continuity of our traditions to my daughters by recreating that special atmosphere made possible only when you are seated around a table with those you love.'

With these unpretentious words we are drawn into a childhood so happy, so privileged, so overflowing with good food and drink, that to not recreate it would be a sacrilege. Raffaela describes herself as a reformed economist; I would describe her as a born-again gastronomist. With her hands and heart she transfers her vision of how a life should be lived to her own children, and with this book passes some of it on to us. *The Fragrance of Basil* is written with profound love and respect for family, tradition and the memory of food. If you lose your food culture then you lose your past, and if you don't know where you came from, you don't know who you are. It appears this family did nothing but eat, and how they found the time to acquire a university education is beyond me. Raffaela has been truly, madly, deeply in love with food and cooking since she suckled her mother's breast milk. Her little daughters love cooking, and they already know how to make bread and pasta – I know this because they have cooked for me.

The recipes in this book are simple and traditional, instructions are razor sharp and all information is extremely well researched, with a comprehensive glossary. When I read the passage on risotto, my taste-buds were so provoked that I raised myself from my couch in the middle of the afternoon and set to cooking her risotto right there and then. I was very interested to read that risotto was originally made with ox marrow. Remembering I had some duck fat in the freezer I made it with that, resulting in great unctuousness and richness of texture if I may say so. Or what about the aranzada made by the steeping, blanching, toasting, slic-ing and cooking of orange rind, almonds and honey together till they are thick and dry and you are salivating and melting?

Raffaela not only knows about food; she describes local customs, songs, prayers and scenery with great detail and nostalgia. Only in Italy are we treated to ostentatious miracles such as the liquefaction of the blood of San Gennaro. An ampoule of his dried blood is kept in the Naples Cathedral, and every year for a brief time it becomes liquid, the archbishop raising it up to the faithful to show the blood-streaked glass.

The secret heroine of this story, however, is the wonderful, exuberant, passionate Mirella, Raffaela's mother. It is she who imbued this family with such a love of life, *gustare* (to taste, using all your senses) and devotion to onion soup, the *meini* biscuits eaten at *merenda* (afternoon tea), eating apple pips and the belief that good lobster should taste of almond.

If you believe food is love, and that beauty and goodness are found in simplicity, then this book is for you.

Peta Mathias

INTRODUCTION

The sweet smell of home

Cooking is the only art form in which I will admit to possessing some talent. It is also the subtle thread which unites my diverse family as well as the only proven method of communicating the continuity of our traditions to my daughters by recreating that special atmosphere made possible only when you are seated around a table with those you love.

Born last century, my grandmother Modesta came from a Modenese peasant family who, while having enough to live on, could hardly have been described as well off. In all peasant families, each member had their own particular responsibility, assigned while they were still very young. When just fifteen, she was married to Gastone, the grandfather whom I never knew and who clearly did not play a dominant role in the family since no one ever spoke of him. My grandmother had a remarkable sense of humour, which she made good use of when describing the notable

events of her life, such as her wedding night, when she ran
horrified from the unexpected encounter which she thought
appropriate to recount when I asked her where children came
from. She never really let on much more, but I am led to believe
that grandfather Gastone must have had some good qualities,
especially since he was a native of Arezzo in Tuscany, a city
famous for being the birthplace of men of culture and charm. In
any case my grandmother made a virtue of necessity and gave
birth to three children, Aldo, Luciana and sixteen years later,
Luigi, my father, whom everyone called Nini – a nickname which
means 'little' in Emilian dialect.

Modesta was also the youngest in the family – hence her
nickname, Modestina, which subsequently became shortened to
just Tina. As the youngest she was not much help in the heavy
work of the fields, and so she became entrusted with the cooking
from a time when she was still too small to be able to comfortably
reach the tabletop, and so in order to work the pasta she had to
stand on a chair. If truth be told, I believe this was due rather to
the family's tendency to short stature than a result of her youth.
Everything that in the course of time I have learned about cooking
by attending professional cooking schools, she knew through
direct experience.

I'm not sure exactly how old I was as far as my first memory
of *nonna* Tina is concerned, but I was definitely younger than
seven because the memory is associated with the house which we
moved from just before my eighth birthday. The kitchen was not
very well lit, with dark oak furniture, a red Formica table and
brown chairs. They were the same type of chairs which now
feature in interior design shops but which were hardly designer
pieces in the seventies. It must have been late afternoon or perhaps
a rainy day. The white glass lamp in the kitchen was not on, and it
was a little gloomy. My grandmother was seated on a chair at the
corner of the table with her back to the windows. She held the
knife in her left hand – she was left-handed like me, but I have

been brought up to use the right hand – and was slicing the onion which she held with the other hand. She raised the slices of onion to her mouth with the knife. I was not surprised by this sight one bit. Children are not surprised by what they see for the first time, they simply take note. I sat myself on her lap and waited for her to give me a piece of onion. I don't remember whether I liked it or not, but even now I still experience a strong emotion when I relive that moment of intimacy with my grandmother.

THE FAMILY TREE

SANTINI FAMILY

Nonno Gastone ♥ Nonna Tina

Zia Luciana

Zio Piero

Daniela — Mariella

Zio Aldo — Nini

♥

Giudi — Raffaela

ALIPRANDI FAMILY

Nonno Innocente ♥ Nonna Elsa

Mirella

Zia Lilia

Zia Mary

♥

Giulia — Martha — Paolo Delmonte

? 2002

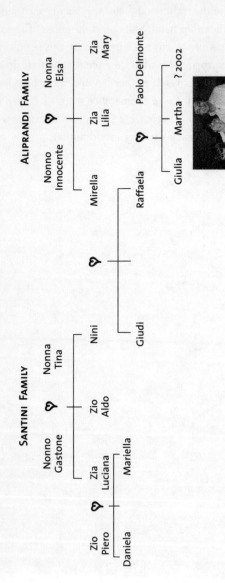

CHAPTER ONE

The house in Via Dino Compagni

My grandmother, mother and father and I all lived in Milan at Number 2, Via Dino Compagni. In Italy the streets are named after writers, poets, historians and patriots. If the idea behind this practice is to perpetuate their memory, the reality is that these names only ever relate to an urban location and not to a highly significant artistic or historic memory. And in any case we only ever remember the surnames: Via Mazzini, Porta Garibaldi. But for me, Via Compagni refers to a person, Dino Compagni. I never knew who he was, but I really was quite kindly disposed towards him. Our place was a modest red brick building of the postwar period, rather dark, with five floors. We lived on the fourth floor. There was only one entrance that opened onto a square room that led to all the rooms in the house – the living room, the kitchen, the bathroom, my parents' room and my grandmother's room. The entranceway seemed larger than it was thanks to a big antique

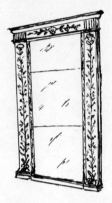

mirror that came from my mother's family home. The mirror had been made according to an antique process, with the result that the reflected image, instead of being clear, seemed to be wrapped in the same haze which accompanies dream images. The mirror had a white and gold stucco frame and took up an entire wall. A wall of sandblasted glass led into the living room, another square room, larger and better lit than the others. Two threadbare armchairs covered in floral fabric stood beside the fireplace. A low chest of drawers with clean lines and steel handles, unmistakably of seventies design, the oval wooden table that had belonged to my mother's family and which we sat around so often over the years in order to celebrate the most important family occasions, and at the rear of the room, the first television I can recall. Small, black, with a convex screen. Not terribly interesting and only ever on for soccer games. Strange, I don't remember my father being that much of a fan. At least, not in hindsight.

My parents' room had French doors which opened out onto a narrow but long balcony. It was a stirring sight to look from the tops of the horse chestnut trees down below to the small Piazza Leonardo da Vinci, in the middle of which I could see my friend the petrol station attendant decked out in his red and grey overalls, the uniform of Esso Petrol. He used to give me all sorts of promotional gimmicks, cards, marbles and sometimes a key ring. I can also remember the noise of our neighbour Mr Rossi's Mini Minor. He was the father of my first best friend, Daria.

Her house was big, with a long corridor that led to the bedrooms, Daria's small room and the large one belonging to her brothers, Fabio and Marcello, who were always dressed in those funny Tyrolese shorts. Mrs Rossi was German. I remember her in the kitchen with one of the most incredible ironing machines that

I can ever recall seeing. One of those professional ones that looks like an old bread toaster. The ones that you open, place the slices of bread, or in this case the shirts in, and then close it and after a few minutes the shirts are ironed or the bread is toasted.

We were inseparable. We attended the same primary school, Leonardo da Vinci, and often returned home together on foot, Daria, Fabio and I. My mother would later describe Fabio as my first 'crush'. She would also refer to Paolo as a crush, right up to the time he became my husband.

When my sister Giuditta was born, soon to be called Giudi, we swooped on the chance to play 'mummy', entertaining that living doll until she would start to cry for help. At that point we would relinquish the baby to the loving ministrations of my mother and run over to Daria's for a snack, which was never withheld. Mrs Rossi would put brown bread, butter, *speck* and cheese on the table. And finally, to complete the meal there would be an unforgettably rich chocolate cake.

I slept in my grandmother's room, in the large bed, and she allowed me to watch *Carosello*. *Carosello* is most definitely emblematic of the childhood of the majority of Italians who grew up

Left: With my proud Dad, three months old.
Right: At the beach, three years old.

in the sixties and seventies, when television programmes were not interrupted by advertisements, which were instead shown together in a single advertising break of ten minutes at the end of the evening news programme. This ad break was called *Carosello*. It was composed of a series of short comic sketches performed by famous actors, played out in brief at a time when the whole family including the children were gathered together around the television. Now *Carosello* enjoys cult status and it is possible to review the most famous ads on the Internet. In all Italian houses where children were present, one would hear, '. . . after *Carosello*, off to bed!'

They became legends, the *carmensita*, a Moka coffee maker with long plaits, in love with Miguel, another Moka, moustachioed with a large sombrero and poncho, ready to defend the good name of coffee which is now world famous. It comes to mind to describe Miguel's poncho as 'multicoloured', and yet the television then was only black and white. In those days perhaps there was more room for fantasy.

Then there was Ringo, cowboy of the blazing south, only placated by corned beef in a can, which was briefly adopted in Italy as a direct result of the pressure brought to bear by children who had made Ringo one of their idols. The natural consequence of the programme was the interest shown by children when it was time to do the grocery shopping.

I can still feel my excitement at going into the first supermarket that opened near home, with all the products that I knew so well on the shelves. Thanks to *Carosello* the supermarket remains for me to this day a place of entertainment and curiosity, feelings which many of my friends share. In my early days working as a business consultant, when it was still pleasurable to leave the office after eight o'clock in the evening, I would stop at the supermarket that I had remained faithful to since childhood and do my shopping with other professionals, men and women in equal numbers, recognisable by their dress and the ever-present briefcase. They all seemed to be enjoying that moment of the day. Watching them I could see them as children, in their cartoon pyjamas, with toothpaste still at the corners of their mouths as they ran to mum, dad, grandma and grandpa, with *Carosello*'s introductory music issuing forth from the television.

This is how my interest in gastronomy began, by means of my exposure to the television and the fragrant nuances of onion. Alongside a purposeful study of flavours disassembled into their basic components, I was able to begin experimenting with the more complex and mass-produced products in the supermarkets.

I do love onions and my mother makes a fantastic onion soup. Over the years I have modified the recipe. I have made it more sophisticated by serving it in a *michetta* – a *la michetta* soft white bread roll. The main distinguishing feature of the *michetta* is that it is completely hollowed out. A good *michetta* should be devoid of nearly all the soft part of the bread and this is only made possible

la michetta

by the use of steam at two specific moments, when the *michetta* has first been put into the oven and when it first starts to rise. Because of its shape, which resembles a rose with open petals, outside Milan it is sometimes called a *rosetta*.

To serve my onion soup, I cut the *michetta's* 'hat' off then pop the rest of the *michetta* into a hot oven to bake until hard. Then, prior to serving, I line the inside of it with slices of Emmental or Gruyère cheese, pour in the piping hot onion soup, and replace the 'hat'.

MY MOTHER'S ONION SOUP

4 large onions
50g butter
1 litre vegetable broth
100g Emmental (or Gruyère) cheese
toasted (or oven grilled) bread slices (country-style or *ciabatta*)
black pepper
wine vinegar

The best onions for this recipe are the white ones, but only if they are in season, when they are fresh and sweet. Alternatively, use the common brown skin or 'blond' type. Just leave them to soak a little longer in the vinegar and water solution. I have even experimented using red onions, where I added a teaspoon of curry powder at the end of cooking. The result was quite different and delicious.

My mother maintains that it's important to slice the onions wafer thin, but then again she has more time on her hands.

Anyhow, a good way of ensuring that the soup doesn't end up with an unpleasant bitter aftertaste and doesn't keep repeating on you is to soak the sliced onions in a solution of water and vinegar for at least an hour. Drain them, then rinse them under running water, then transfer them to a large frypan containing melted butter.

The secret of a good onion soup lies in the cooking of the onions; they have to 'melt', as we say in jargon. The flame must be very low and the onions must cook until transparent and glossy. When they have totally lost their initial consistency, cover with the vegetable stock and simmer for about an hour, covered, at low heat. Check the consistency frequently; it should be creamy and not too liquid.

Line the base of an ovenproof soup terrine with the bread slices.

Pour in the soup and cover with finely sliced cheese and a good sprinkling of freshly ground black pepper. Place the terrine in the oven and grill until golden brown. Serve immediately.

The first recipe that I ever learned was *crema pasticcera*, which my grandmother used to make for my *merenda*[1] when she had fresh eggs, laid that day. She didn't weigh the ingredients, she wouldn't dream of it, just made a rough estimate based on experience.

NONNA TINA'S CREMA PASTICCERA

For each person allow:
1 egg yolk
half an eggshell filled with sugar
1 tablespoon flour
1/2 glass milk
lemon peel

Mix together the yolk and sugar, add the flour, mix well, then add milk gradually. Add lemon peel, heat and bring to the boil. Cook for exactly three minutes from the start of boiling. If cooked any longer the crema will curdle. If cooked for less, it will taste of flour.

---

1   Merenda – a snack either sweet or savoury in the late afternoon that fills the gap until the evening meal, which is usually eaten around 8 after shops and offices have closed. A whole food industry revolves around snack food for merenda.

During my first cooking course this version of the recipe was the subject of numerous ironic smiles. But on the explicit request of Fabio Zago, the chef at the Italian Cooking Institute who teaches the beginners, I had the pleasure of demonstrating, scales in hand, that popular wisdom is also expressed in the art of cooking. My two favourite moments in the day are the *merenda* and the *aperitivo* or cocktail hour. Both are uniquely and typically Italian, having evolved on account of our daily timetable which seems crazy to the outside world. Breakfast – in the peasant traditions of the past, a meal of polenta and meat or bread and salami washed down by a good wine – has been for years now just a short black coffee. We have been inundated by biscuits resembling little sandwiches and animal-shaped cereal, but for the most part the grown-ups still stick to just having a coffee for breakfast.

From the beginning of pre-school for children from three years on, lunch becomes increasingly an opportunity to introduce them to the culture of the table and to a variety of tastes as well as to the joys of conviviality. My daughter Giulia spent her first year of pre-school in a state school in Milan. During the hour in which lunch was served, which concluded with the daily ritual of teeth cleaning, they would lay the small round tables with tablecloths and cutlery and play at waiting on tables in turns. At the school entrance on a blackboard propped up by a small bear, the day's menu would appear, carefully prepared with the aim of delivering just the right nutritional value as well as relieving mothers of the burden of an equally complete dinner.

The memory of the school dining hall of the 'Orsoline' Sisters that I attended for more than thirteen years has faded, as has the memory of the limp and plain pasta with butter and cheese, followed by a small slice of veal or chicken, accompanied by beans, peas or carrots. The dining hall was huge, completely filled by long tables, set with tablecloths, napkins and a small *michetta* or child's portion for each table companion. From the dining hall you could enter the garden by passing through the wide glass doors, but during the long winter months the sky remained overcast and still for weeks and very little light filtered through. As if to make up for it, the babble of voices inside was deafening, so much so that it was only possible to communicate with the schoolmate right next to you. What does remain, however, is the intense pleasure I felt in sharing these simple meals with my school friends, especially when once a week, the nuns in their black habits and white sleeve covers and aprons, would serve vanilla, strawberry or even chocolate pudding instead of the usual fruit.

Merenda, the snack before the evening meal, belongs above all to childhood and, thank heaven, also to motherhood when one always has a good excuse for eating. As a child the most exciting thing about being invited to play at a friend's house was *merenda* time. A true ritual, it could not be missed and if by chance it wasn't forthcoming, I would take swift action and ask for it, in that way so typical of children. Italian children are particularly good at it. 'M-u-m . . . I'm h-u-n-g-r-y . . .' they whisper in their mother's ear, not quietly as they have been taught is good manners, but in such a way that the hostess is sure to hear. The child's mother protests unconvincingly, but the trap is set and the lady of the house is unable to refuse a bite to eat to a hungry child. This ritual would be repeated in every home we visited. It never mattered how many *merende* you had already eaten. Nowadays I wonder if it is a character trait my daughters have inherited, one of those things associated with being Italian.

But it was most definitely the birthday party which laid claim to the most gluttonous *merenda* of all.

Birthdays were celebrated with all due ceremony. We would be dressed in embroidered frocks, with our best shoes and bows in our hair, ready and waiting for the whipped cream, *crema pasticcera* and chocolate to come, as we set off with a beautifully wrapped gift and our mother's advice not to make ourselves sick on sweet things. In our house, sweets and cakes were reserved for special occasions, birthday parties, baptisms, weddings and communions.

It's not me but this is a typical expression of any child before such a feast.

Simple apple cakes would be prepared to be eaten at *merenda* time, but birthday cakes were something else altogether. They were beautifully decorated, multicoloured, with delicious fillings – most often a sponge cake infused with fruit juice, filled with *crema pasticcera* and then covered with whipped cream and decorated as each occasion dictated, chocolate hail for birthdays and little silver balls for baptisms. As well as the birthday cake, there would be *pasticcini* or pastries, *bignet* or cream puffs filled with *crema pasticcera* or chocolate, little tarts with fresh strawberries or blueberries, dainty little meringue mushrooms coated with dark chocolate. But my favourites are still to this day *cannoncini*, little tubes of puff pastry filled with *crema pasticcera*. Paolo attended a *pasticceria mignon* – a patisserie course – in order to be able to satisfy this passion of mine, shared enthusiastically by my daughters. The recipe itself is straightforward. The sheets of puff pastry found at the supermarket will do just fine. The preparation is a bit time-consuming and you need *bussolotti*, empty steel tubes 10cm long around which you wrap the 1cm wide strips of puff pastry in spirals. The still uncooked *cannoncini* are sprinkled with icing sugar and baked in the oven at 200°C for around 10–15 minutes until they become a light golden colour. Once they have cooled down they are easy to detach from the steel tubes and are ready to be filled with *crema pasticcera*.

Apart from the sweet things at parties, there were always small white bread rolls, filled with cooked or plain ham, little pizzas, puff pastry savouries and rectangles of *focaccia*.

Even if we don't call it *merenda* anymore, around 4 o'clock in the afternoon Italians are assailed by hunger pangs that make us abandon our desks or interrupt our work. Those of us who are watching their weight make do with a coffee, or perhaps a cracker – now I understand why when sweet crackers were introduced they never took off – or a biscuit. Others, like my husband, Paolo, and I, for example, prefer an ice-cream. Italian *gelaterie* produce ice-cream non-stop, made from fresh fruit and milk that mothers buy for *merenda*, as well as sugarless ice-cream, but what pleasure is there in that?

In the weekends spent out of town, *merenda* once more assumes an important role, as in the autumnal chestnut roastings. Everyone is equipped with a wicker basket as they venture into the forests gathering chestnuts. Then it is good practice to make an incision in the chestnuts so that they don't explode during the cooking process, when they are put into specially designed iron pots with holes in the bottom and placed over the fire in the fireplace. The chestnuts should really be left to dry for a few days, spread out on the floor of the house, but if you have small children this can be dangerous, especially because of the worms that you find in them. In different seasons of the year my mother's house is filled with fruit lying on benches and on the spacious floor area of the entranceway, left to ripen like *nespole* – loquats – or left to dry out like nuts at the beginning of summer or chestnuts in autumn. Giulia was ten months old and she couldn't believe her luck at finding all those little balls to play with. Our only concern was that she not put them in her mouth and we didn't notice that she was far more interested in a fat and appealing worm peering out from a chestnut. But Giulia had most definitely noticed it. It is

nespole

well known that at that age curiosity is
satisfied orally. Sunday, the day after, I
found a nice fat worm in her nappy
and decided to keep it to show the
paediatrician, convinced that she had
been eating earth and as a result had
worms. On Monday morning I took
the still frozen specimen to the paediatrician
who prescribed an intensive series of tests until
Anna Maria, her midwife, was seized by doubt. 'Wasn't it possible
that she might have eaten the worm?' Reconstructing past events,
it didn't take much to reach that conclusion, to the huge relief of
those who would have been involved in the collection of samples.
Giulia still loves chestnuts.

castagne

My grandmother spent most of
her day in the kitchen. But my
memories of her cooking belong
to a later time. My memories of
the house are associated with its
tranquil silence, the big bed which
I slept in with my grandmother,
the *merenda* of onion we shared,
and food such as *passatelli* and *gli
uccelletti infilzati*.

I once believed that *passatelli*
were an invention of my grandmother to induce me to eat soup,

Nonna Tina

but I subsequently discovered them to be a real speciality in the
cooking tradition of the Emilia region, with many variations. A
typical dish of peasant families, whose subsistence diet consisted
of products readily available on the farm, *passatelli* are a quick and
tasty dish making use of ingredients that can always be found in
the fridge.

PASSATELLI

passatelli tool

2 eggs
salt, pepper and a little grated nutmeg
lemon peel
100g Parmigiano Reggiano or Grana Padano,
   grated finely
80g breadcrumbs (white bread, no crusts)
1.5 litres of good broth

In a bowl, beat the eggs together with a pinch of nutmeg, the finely grated peel (use a cheese grater) of half a lemon and a pinch of salt.

Add the grated Parmigiano Reggiano and the breadcrumbs and mix to a smooth dough. Put the dough through a potato ricer (or froth skimmer with large holes) held over a pot containing the hot broth. After giving it a good stir, the delicious smelling, wholesome soup is ready.

A special utensil called a *passatelli* iron is usually used. It comprises a robust metal disk 15cm in diameter, slightly convex, with 5mm holes. It has a bar mounted on it with handles at either end. The *passatelli* dough is turned out onto a large wooden board and the iron is placed on top and pressed until vermicelli are passed through the holes. They are then cut to 4–5cm lengths and thrown into the boiling broth.

In 1999, the Italian Cooking Academy ran a competition in order to identify the best recipe for *passatelli*. There were six winning recipes, chosen from among recipe books, cooking texts, and grandmothers' notebooks. The result of the placings struck me because it was symbolic of Italian gastronomic culture whose roots are based in tradition, but which demonstrates a constant and speedy evolution towards a modern cuisine, admitting new flavours. The rules required the compulsory use of three basic ingredients – breadcrumbs, Parmigiano Reggiano and eggs, but

allowed for variations in quantity and in the herbs and spices used. I thus discovered that my grandmother's recipe, which took second place, came from one of the most well-known Italian cooking texts, *The Science of Cooking and the Art of Eating Well*, better known as *L'Artusi*, after the author's name, Pellegrino Artusi. It was first published in 1891, with fifty editions in print by 1954. This recipe calls for ox marrow – not terribly digestible or easily conserved even when it does come from a healthy and verifiable source – the upshot of which is that making *passatelli* according to this recipe requires in-depth planning and research. The recipe that won was representative of the evolution of taste towards increasingly more complex flavours, in this case achieved with the addition of finely chopped parsley, which is equally delicious. Among the other recipes, one replaced parsley with chopped walnuts and another with lemon rind.

One of the many reasons which has motivated me over the years to go to evening classes at the Italian Cooking Institute is the idea that cooking is a creative art and no less important than other art forms. Once you have learnt the basic techniques, in most part the same in all culinary traditions, there is no more to the art of cooking than giving free rein to one's creativity. I think the reason why I remember the following recipe so well is because of its name, *uccelletti infilʒati* – little birds impaled on a skewer. It is also an Emilian recipe, even if it appears in many other Italian regions with different names, 'little birds rolled up', or even on toothpicks, or bound together with cooking twine. The main idea is to bring out the flavour of the *fettina*, which is the same as schnitzel but almost always veal, by using the stronger flavour of the cheese and ham. There are limitless variations. I don't know if the Italian Cooking Academy has already noted it as being worthwhile, but as far as I am concerned I would suggest a national contest for this recipe. My grandmother would allow me to stuff the *fettine* with pieces of raw ham and Parmesan, having already tenderised the meat with a meat tenderiser or *batticarne*.

Today there are more sophisticated versions but back then this was composed of a heavy steel disc, 10cm in diameter, with a short steel handle welded to the centre of the disc. Together we rolled the *fettine* and pierced them with toothpicks. It is a perfect recipe for introducing children to cooking. They can't hurt themselves or dirty the kitchen with flour, chocolate or other ingredients, and most of the time having completed the preparation, they have already dined on cheese and ham. Nowadays I roll the *fettine* in a sage leaf, partly because it adds a pleasant taste and partly because this variation has provided me with the excuse needed to change their name – which always seemed macabre to me – to 'little birds in clothes'. In spring I stuff them with cheese and a piece of fresh artichoke, in autumn with a tiny slice of white truffle, stolen from the unforgettable *tajarin*, a local variation of fresh tagliatelle with truffle, produced near Andrea and Patrizia's house in Monticello d'Alba in Monferrato, where you can buy a truffle without raising a mortgage. Monferrato is a hilly area of the Piemonte region that often becomes cloaked in a fog so light but

truffle slicer

persistent that it seems to penetrate the earth. The air is always heavy with humidity and I believe that these are the optimum conditions under which these funny fungi that cost a fortune develop. It certainly is a paradise for those who love mushrooms, truffles and hazelnuts. One of the recipes of ancient local tradition, *il bonet*, is a pudding made with melted dark chocolate, crushed *amaretti* biscuits and flavoured with rum, perfect for finishing a meal with a flourish.

GLOSSARY:

MICHETTA (mee-ket-ta) is a bread typically found in Milan, a small bread roll, *panino* (one portion), made with dough that has been left to rise for a reasonable length of time. Its hexagonal shape is created by passing the dough through a special mould.

PARMIGIANO REGGIANO DOP (Protected Designation of Origin) is probably the best-known cheese in Italy and abroad. Its territory of origin encompasses the provinces of Modena, Reggio Emilia and Parma and part of the provinces of Bologna and Mantova. The milk used for Parmigiano is collected and brought to the dairies twice a day. Milk from the evening milking is put into broad, shallow troughs so that the cream rises to the surface. The following morning the cream is removed and skimmed milk is mixed with whole milk from the morning milking and transferred into truncated cone-shaped vats. The mixture is then inoculated with milk enzymes obtained by allowing the previous day's whey to sour naturally. Next it is heated to 33–34°C and rennet is added. The soft curd is then cut up finely into lentil-sized granules before being heated to about 55°C and transferred to moulds, salted for about 24 days then left to mature for at least 12 months, but this process may go on for much longer.

SPECK is a specialty of Trentino-Alto Adige. The pork belly is slowly smoked over beech wood with herbs then airdried for a long time. Used for wrapping lean meat in order to keep it moist and give flavour during cooking, it is traditionally served as as an *antipasto* with the local dark rye bread.

TAJARIN (tah-ee-ah-reen) is a pasta typical of the Piemonte region – thin hand-cut *tagliatelle* which is usually served during autumn with fresh white truffles and grated Parmesan cheese.

CHAPTER TWO

The smell of snow

Travelling from Milan to Lecco, the point of departure is Viale Fulvio Testi, straight and wide and seemingly never-ending, full of traffic lights, all synchronised so that if you take off on the green light and maintain a constant speed, you will get all the successive green lights. But there is always too much traffic and this trick only worked if we left really late on the Friday night. Then we would take the motorway, which was invariably blocked by the endless roadworks, to Lecco, a city with the waters of Lake Lario, commonly known as Lake Como, lapping at its edges.

The unmistakable Mount Resegone rises up behind Lecco, the mountain's name meaning 'large saw' in the Lombard dialect, due to the shape of its jagged peaks. This hilly zone from Milan to Lake Como is called Brianza, even though it is not a distinct geographic area and the borders are not clearly determined. Here you will find the elaborately decorated old villas of landowners, *cascine*,[1] homes and places of work belonging to peasant families, but above all the roots of Lombard cooking which are deeply embedded in poverty and in the history of the scourge of pellagra. It is an agricultural zone, once famous for the cultivation of mulberries and for silk and corn production. The peasant diet was based on corn meal which was used for making polenta or for large loaves of bread, often only partially cooked due to their sheer volume, or *minestrone* of rice, legumes and vegetables usually flavoured with *lardo*. The only condiments were salt, rape oil and, on rare occasions, butter. Eggs were hardly ever eaten because the peasants preferred to sell them to make a few *lire*, while meat only made an appearance for religious festivals. The few head of cattle, found only in the hill areas, made it possible for the peasant diet to be enriched with milk and a little cheese. The grain was plentiful, but packed as it was into damp and poorly aerated bedrooms, frequently went rotten.

maize for polenta

Nowadays for Italians *polenta* is an opportunity to celebrate, especially when it is eaten with cold milk or fresh cream as my mother likes it, with eggs or butter and *porcini* mushrooms *trifolati* – thinly sliced and cooked with oil, garlic and parsley – as I prefer it, or with sausages and cheese, the way it is often prepared in the alpine huts.

But for the peasants, it was the only food eaten all day, hunger's constant companion, because even though it fills the stomach, it is not very nourishing. Maize lacks the essential amino acids, above all niacin, an indispensable vitamin for metabolic function, whose deficiency causes pellagra, a deadly illness associated with poverty, only

---

1 Dairy farms.

discovered in the 1900s, and whose cure consists in a variation of diet.

It would eventually be discovered that this vital niacin was also present in maize when it was subjected to a simple process – washing. Originally from Latin America, maize was introduced into Italy in the 1500s where it became know as *grano turco* – literally, Turkish maize, a term used in those days for everything which had a foreign or unknown origin. What's more, the American Indians, despite eating a diet of mainly maize, were strangers to pellagra. Polenta was unknown to them and maize was warmed up in water, rinsed and then ground in order to make bread. Somehow, whether by luck or experimentation, we will never know, the American Indians learned to handle maize, while we paid dearly for the mistake of introducing a new food source into our alimentary regime without also embracing its culture of origin.

In 1830 in a Lombardy which at the time could count two million inhabitants, the number of sick was around 20,000. When, in the second half of the 1800s, the golden age of the silk industry came to an unexpected end as a consequence of the competition from Asian production, an outpouring of protest against the unfair contracts imposed by the landowners became inevitable.

By the end of the 1700s agricultural production was no longer able to satisfy the needs of a population in continual growth and so it gave way gradually to manufacturing activity such as cotton production and above all to woodwork, which in turn gave rise to the proliferation of furniture factories, which to this day still constitute the principal manufacturing industry of the Brianza region.

The lake scenery of Lecco and its surroundings, damp and cloaked in autumnal fog, is featured in the works of many painters, including Leonardo da Vinci, who seems to have been inspired by it for the setting of his *Mona Lisa*. I recognised the small town from afar, by its threadlike neon lights, which illuminated the landscape; whether leaving for or returning from the weekend, we often passed there after sunset. If we left with our mother immediately after school we would arrive at Lecco in time for *merenda*. The obligatory stop was a bakery on the lakeside whose name I never knew, but was easy to find just by following the aroma of freshly baked bread and above all of *meini* and of *ossi da mordere*[2] in November.

In the Milanese tradition, these large elongated biscuits were prepared on 23 April, St George's Day, and eaten with liquid cream and milk. They are made with maize flour and white flour, but old Lombard recipe books record that they were once made with millet, which gave them their original name of *pan di mei*, millet bread. In my research on Lombard culinary traditions I have found endless variations, and by taking elements from one recipe and adding it to another, I have produced my favourite version, which is memorable not just because of the taste, but because of their aroma when they have just come out of the oven, which transports me back to that bakery on the shores of Lake Como.

2   Literally 'bones to gnaw on'.

MEINI BISCUITS

20g fresh yeast, or a sachet of dry active yeast
150g white flour
150g finely ground corn meal (*Fioretto* variety)
100g coarsely ground corn meal (*Bramata* variety)
150g sugar
3 eggs
120g butter
1/2 glass milk
2 tablespoons Sambuco – elder flowers (In Italy the fresh wild variety
    can be found in springtime or they are available in the dry version
    from herbalist shops under the name of *Panigada*). You can
    substitute with 2 tablespoons of fennel seeds.

Dissolve the yeast in 3 tablespoons of tepid water. Sift the flours into a
bowl. Add the sugar, whole eggs and yeast. Mix well, then incorporate
the softened butter, milk and elder flowers (or fennel seeds). The dough
should be soft at this stage. If not, add a touch more milk.

Shape dough into a ball and place to rest for about 2 hours in a lightly
oiled bowl, covered with plastic film.

Make little balls from the dough, then flatten them till a 10cm
diameter disc is obtained. Place on a greased baking tray and brush with
an egg yolk wash and finish off with a sprinkle of icing sugar. Bake in a
preheated oven at 180°C for 20–30 minutes. Dust with more icing sugar
and serve the *meini* warm with some liquid cream or milk.

Ossi da mordere are a strictly Lombard recipe, traditionally served
on 2 November, the day of the Commemoration of the Dead, and
still found today in all the bakeries and cake shops for the whole
month of November. My mother comes from a family of pure-
blooded Milanesi, whose roots can be traced back as far as the

My parents on their honeymoon in the Alps in 1962.

1200s – her surname, Aliprandi, certifies Milanese origin, just like a good wine. Then my father arrived on the scene, born in Milan, his mother from Emilia and father from Tuscany, to corrupt the family bloodline according to my mother's version, or to make it stronger, bringing new and more vigorous blood, according to my father's. In any case, my mother is a reliable source when it comes to authentic Milanese traditions. But not, it would seem, as far as *ossi da mordere* are concerned. What my mother calls *ossi da mordere*, my research shows instead to be *pan dei morti* – bread of the dead, a sweet bread, also prepared on 2 November, dark in colour and with a soft consistency, made with flour, cocoa, dried fruit, wine, egg whites and flavoured with cinnamon. In the past, flour was substituted with the left-over crumbs of other cakes. Characteristic of the *pan dei morti* was their method of being cooked on *ostie*.[3] They taste a bit like gingerbread, *rob de sciuri*[4] – rich man's bread. *Ossi da mordere* are instead large elongated biscuits, white in colour with an extremely hard consistency, but brittle, and their shape and colour resemble bones. In a famous restaurant in Monza they were served with a red wine called *Sangue di Giuda* – Judas' Blood produced in Oltrepo' pavese, just

---

3   *Ostie* are hosts in religious usage, but in baking terms are thin wafers like rice paper. Also used to cover *torrone*.

4   Milanese dialect expression meaning a custom, habit of the well off or *cose da signori*.

beyond the border with Pavia, a viticulture region below the Po river. And so understandably I decided on a name change and in my recipe they are called *duri da mordere*, hard to bite.

DURI DA MORDERE

200g peeled almonds
100g sugar
150g white flour
lemon peel
1 egg white

The correct procedure calls for the almonds and sugar to be crushed together in a mortar, as only in this way can the sugar absorb the perfumed oil of the almonds. But I'm quite happy to use a blender to briefly mix the two together.

Place the flour, blended almonds/sugar and lemon peel in a large bowl. Give them a good mix, then delicately add the whipped (to peaks) egg white.

Shape the dough, which at this stage is fairly dry, into a long *salame* and cut it into ¹/₂ cm slices. Lay the *salame* slices onto a baking tray lined with baking paper and bake in a preheated oven at 170°C for about 40–50 minutes. Serve them once cooled. They keep for ages.

The Italian alpine range called Alpi includes valleys that have been inhabited for centuries because they are a point for border crossings, and as such were sites of strategic importance as well as being areas favoured by settlement due to the tall Alpi that slope down into lovely valleys. The people who have inhabited these valleys for centuries have a unique identity shaped by the difficulty of communicating with other inhabited areas during the long months of winter, and manifest the effects of foreign influences – from Switzerland, France and Austria.

Via Chiavenna

From Lecco to Colico the road flanks the lake and at Colico, where the river Adda runs into the lake, it forks with one branch leading to Valtellina and the other to Val Chiavenna, whose main town centre is Chiavenna, 10km from the Swiss border. The name originates from the word *chiave*, key, alluding to its position of strategic access to the mountain passes of Maloja and Spluga, which either block, or admit, foreign invasions.

But the name could also come from the Latin word meaning debris, which is left by the Mera river that passes through the city of Chiavenna, sited on the flood banks and into which the huge glaciers have over the years deposited millions of square metres of rock. What remains of this enormous erosive phenomenon is known as the Marmitte dei Giganti,[5] which takes its name from a

---

5   The Giant's Cauldron Nature Reserve.

term used by geologists to describe the glacial origins of these enormous potholes.

Twenty thousand years ago, the water carried debris along until it reached a fissure into which it fell and as a result of the erosive action, the rock became scooped out creating different shapes including dish-like forms or the potholes that give the reserve its name. These naturally smooth and hollow rocks are clearly visible in the park and their dimensions vary from three metres in diameter and twelve metres in depth. The *massi erratici*, erratic boulders, are so named because having broken away from the distant rock masses they have been carried by the glaciers like floating bodies until they come to rest on these rocks. They are easily recognisable because they are of an entirely different colour and composition to the local rock.

Making my way easily along the path, I remember experiencing a moment of pleasure mixed with wonder, a kind of reawakening of the senses and harmony with nature. The fresh night air had become effervescent with a breeze which seemed to play between the smooth and striated rocks of an almost lunar landscape. I then noticed the abundant growth of strange and unique succulents, similar to bonsais, on the rocks, a result of the special micro-climate of the region, which in spite of appearing so innocuous now, bears witness to the power of nature. The ancient inhabitants of the area had also discovered a way to exploit this distinctive smooth and hard green stone known as *pietra ollare* by using it for making pots (*olla* means pot). The special feature of this stone is that it can store heat and release it slowly, making it perfect for a certain type of cooking which needs to be done far away from heat sources, called *sulla pietra* – on the coals.

Natural cavities or grottoes, called *crotti*, have formed as a result of past earthquakes. An air current with a constant temperature of 6–8°C passes though these *crotti* and the Sorel, as it is called, is like the breath of the mountains. The constant temperature makes these grottoes the perfect place for storing salami, cheeses and wine.

Every year in September, on traditional feast days, access to these grottoes is made possible. They become a place where 'good wine is sold and schooling in the humanities is given', according to an inscription dated at the end of the 8th century. Once inside you can try *bresaola*, still handcrafted the traditional way, and the harder to find *violino di capra*, literally goat's violin. *Bresaola* is the meat most typical of the Valtellina without being a true *salame*, made as it is from either beef or deer, devoid of fat and instead of being made into a sausage like a *salame*, dried naturally by being hung outside. *Bresaola* has slightly different characteristics and taste depending on the area of production and the cut of meat used. *Bresaola* from Valchiavenna is a lighter colour and moist, while a variation from Valtellina, *slinẓega*, is slightly dryer with a stronger taste. The *violino di capra* is the dried meat from the goat's hind leg, so named because of the unique way it is sliced, balanced on the shoulder as if it were a violin and using the knife as a bow. It is dark red in colour and has an unmistakable taste.

Ascending by means of devious and frightening hairpin bends you arrive at Madesimo, 1500 metres above sea level, in the high Spluga valley, lush with fir and larch trees, encircled by majestic peaks. The road has been widened and the buses transporting the Sunday skiers most certainly don't encounter any difficulties these days. Thirty years ago it was a long and arduous journey. After the locality of Isola, the road becomes steep with bends that in those days allowed for only one car to pass at a time. From the back seat I could only see snow and those funny icicles that hung down from the entrance of the tunnels and from the rocks that protruded from the inner edge of the road protected by the mountain, which made me feel safe. At that age and even now on long journeys the car would send me to sleep immediately and I would have slept until we arrived at our destination were it not for the constant stops and my mother's toots, or those of the bus driver on his descent from Madesimo. Then I would sit up, but all I could see was snow. My mother advised me to remain horizontal and I didn't mind a bit. In those days you didn't have to wear seatbelts and the back seat was large enough and comfortable enough to be used as a bed for a girl of seven. My nose was frozen, the first part of my body to get cold and the hardest part to warm up again. But the most pleasurable sensation was the smell of the snow and of the dry cold of the mountains in winter.

I recall an occasion when my mother has stopped on the edge of the road but the local bus can't pass. The bus driver hops down and helps my mother to back the car up a little so the bus can squeeze past on its descent, empty, towards Campodolcino. On its ascent it will be full of children on their way back from school. From the edge of the road I can see down into the chasm of the valley. In later years, this sensation of 'being in the mountains', the smell of the snow and ice, no longer surprised me when I would wake in the car, but struck me instead as beautiful when I would exit the well heated interior and find myself in a landscape that was a little spooky, almost unnatural.

We resume our snail-like progress upward around the final bend, under the canopies which shelter you from snowfalls and where the snow chains make an annoying sound on the wet asphalt, only partially covered with snow. The sound of the chains sliding over the compact snow is much more harmonious and already has me anticipating all the games I'm going to play, and above all my father's arrival when I can go skiing with him on the *canalone* of Val di Lei, a slope with a high degree of difficulty, all hills and jumps, described as 'white vertigo' by Dino Buzzati, the famous Italian writer whom I studied at school.

I can barely walk but I can ski with my Dad, Madesimo, 1965.

I can't remember exactly when I learnt to ski, just as I can't remember learning to walk. If I think about it now, it seems as if I have always skied. I can remember, or perhaps I think I can remember, when I look at photos, that my father would carry me on his shoulders down the ski slopes and then he would let go of me and I would slide on my bottom into my mother's arms as she waited just below. My nose is frozen again, and I inhale the smell of the icy cold and everything around me is blindingly white. How wonderful it felt to return to the warm house in that funny modern condominium where *nonna* Tina was waiting for me on the third floor, ready to help me out of my wet ski suit, throw me into a hot bath and then sing me to sleep in her arms while she sang me a *ninna nanna* (lullaby) in dialect.

Ninna nanna, ninna oh, questa bimba a chi la do?
la daro' alla befana che se la tenga una settimana . . .
La daro' alla sua mamma che le canta ninna nanna.

Ninna nanna, ninna oh, to whom should this little baby girl go?
I'll give her for a week to the old Befana[6] . . .
I'll give her to her mother who will sing to her ninna nanna.

I have clear memories of that warm house. My two cousins
Mariella and Daniela have a large-brimmed hat they are both
trying on in front of the mirror. They are very different from each
other. Mariella the eldest is so like her mother my *ʒia* Luciana. Not
very tall, with typically Emilian features, she is really beautiful
with a placid nature. She is married and her son Matteo, three years
my junior, has been my playmate for as long as I can remember.
Daniela is tall and slim, with prominent features, always deeply
tanned, an extrovert with a mischievous personality. I don't see her
often but she has been for years now my favourite cousin. It is in
fact there, in front of that mirror, that I actually discover that they
are sisters.

It was a modern condominium consisting of four or five floors,
built on the banks of the Liro stream. In front of the entrance to
the condominium was a large open space that in those days wasn't
busy with traffic or pedestrians and where we had snowball fights
and used to build snowmen. I can vividly recall the room where I
slept with *nonna* Tina, which had a wardrobe covered with floral
wallpaper in front of the bed. I am there, lying on the bed, trying
to lift off part of the wallpaper with my little finger. My grandmother is nearby and I have a fever. It has been a glorious day,
perhaps a bit much for a small child, or maybe I just didn't feel the
cold. While playing with Eduardo and Matteo I sank knee deep

---

6 The Befana is an ugly old lady, who brings sweets to good children on
6 January and pieces of coal to naughty ones.

Dad, Giudi and me,
Lago di Lecco, 1975.

into fresh snow, and it took them some time to extract me, soaking wet and bone cold. That night I had to be well because it was New Year's Eve and my grandmother would stay home with all the grandchildren and we'd play *tombola* (bingo). I still have the *tombola* box, though some of the numbers have been lost. The counters are on little wooden coasters with red borders and red numbers, kept in a raw jute pouch. The score-cards have large numbers on them and my grandmother gets us to use dried beans to cover the numbers called.

The prize for winning? Lots of sweets. Many years later at Cervinia, on the slopes of Mt Cervino, it is still New Year's Eve and we are going to play *tombola* again, but this time at Gigliola's, a friend's, house. And on the menu is something which will make me remember that evening at Madesimo and which will remain forever fixed in my memories of that time. Gigliola announces it as a big surprise, but I know it well, it is *rotolo verde*.

ROTOLO VERDE

1kg fresh spinach
salt and pepper
nutmeg
100g butter
300g ricotta
80g fresh Parmigiano Reggiano
300g flour
just under a cup of water (180 ml)
a few sage leaves

Prepare the filling by blanching the spinach briefly in boiling salted water then squeezing it well to get rid of all excess water. Season the spinach by putting it in a frying pan with a knob of butter then add salt and grated nutmeg to taste.

When the mixture is cold, combine it with the ricotta and two tablespoons of grated Parmigiano Reggiano.

Mix the flour with as much water as you need to achieve a soft but dry dough. You can use fresh pasta dough, which is made with 300g of flour and three whole eggs. Cover the dough and leave it to stand for 20–30 minutes, then roll it out into a rectangle 20–25cm wide and 2mm thick.

Spread the spinach mixture over the dough with a spatula, taking care to leave about 1cm at the sides free of mixture. Then roll the dough, starting from the shortest side of the rectangle and rolling it reasonably tight, but without pressing too hard.

If they had known about sushi in Modena, I would have advised them to use the same technique! Wrap the roll in a length of cloth a little bigger than the roll itself and tie the two ends with cooking twine as if you were wrapping a sweet. Immerse the roll wrapped in the cloth in lightly boiling salted water and leave it to simmer for 40 minutes. While it is cooking keep checking to make sure that it is always completely immersed, otherwise add more boiling water.

Carefully drain the roll, unwrap it from the cloth and cut it into 1 or 2cm thick pieces depending on your dexterity.

Serve it like this, sprinkled with grated Parmesan and the left-over melted butter and adding the sage leaves, or put the slices in an oven-proof dish, gently layering them, sprinkle with grated Parmesan, butter and sage leaves and put them under the grill for 10 minutes so that they become crispy.

This dish is also delicious reheated.

GLOSSARY:

LARDO (lahr-do) is made from the layer of fat found under the pig's skin, seasoned with salt and pepper and with herbs in some areas. We serve it thinly sliced on rye bread as *antipasto*. It has a very soft texture and a delicate flavour. There are three places in Italy that are particularly famous for their *lardo*. In Colonnata, a village in Tuscany, the *lardo* is cured in huge vats made from the local Carrara marble and seasoned with pepper, whole cloves and rosemary; Arnad, in Valle D'Aosta, produces a slightly different version. Here the *lardo*, without the rind, is seasoned with salt, pepper, herbs, juniper berries and garlic and put in a white wine solution. The English word 'lard' refers to the melted layer of fat found just above the lean part of the meat. This is what we call *strutto*.

CHAPTER THREE

Lunch with my family

Not long after my sister Giuditta was born, we went to live in Via Tunisia, just outside the old walls of the city. The apartment was on the first floor and had previously been the home of my *zia* Luciana, but my father, who owned a building firm, had completely renovated it.

The building had two extremely high doors of wrought iron, a main entrance and a secondary service entrance. The main lift was like all lifts in old buildings, creaky, tiny and slow, requiring a funny little retractable seat that enabled the tenants on the top floors to sit down during the long upward journey. The chair was covered in red velvet and reminded me of the folding seats at the theatre that we call *strapuntino*, which operate on the same principle, allowing for extra seating when all the regular seats are taken. I never had enough time to make use of it but would watch Mrs Fabiola, who had always lived in the building on the seventh floor, get up off the seat with the aid of her walking stick when the lift reached the ground floor. Hair as white as snow, a long nose which bestowed her face with a certain authority, she had a languid expression and pale blue eyes that seemed to be able to see things that were invisible to the rest of us. She would greet me pleasantly enough, but I don't think she ever knew my name.

The first floor landing was always dark, windowless and without any cracks to admit the light, apart from the feeble rays that filtered through the leadlights of an antique door. When the bulb from the wall sconce that was permanently on would blow, you needed a torch or a good memory to put the right key in the right keyhole.

The door to our apartment was reinforced, very modern in dark walnut, and opened into the large living room, divided up into three different living spaces. My father had chosen to lower the ceiling to create a pleasant contrast on entering the apartment (as well as creating a contrast with the rest of the apartment) and the lighting was a successful combination of recessed spotlights in the ceiling and contemporary designer lamps with the odd concession to antiquity, such as the two table lamps which came from my maternal grandmother's house, a white porcelain one with an embossed fruit design and the black one adorned with

The white lamp

figures from Greek mythology and a cream lampshade. The latter sat on a small table with long and finely turned legs made up of blocks of wood of different colours creating an elegant pattern. The table top could be opened out to double its surface area by means of the brass hinges at its four corners, thus providing the unexpected functionality of a card table.

The old card table

The conversation area was furnished with low maroon leather sofas, a huge rectangular glass table with a silverplated trim and iron legs, which accompanies me every time I move house, and a fireplace that never worked. In front of the fireplace my mother had placed a modern firescreen, a simple sheet of smoked glass that rested on two wrought-iron feet. Around the same antique oval wooden table were four padded chairs made out of ochre-coloured velvety material and two of the same design that still had their original black leather covering, attached to the wood frame by big studs. My parents' tastes had always clashed.

My father adored modern interior design, its technology and functionality, while my mother was enamoured of anything antique, without being too concerned with practicalities. But in these surroundings she had really outdone herself. Behind this table she had hung a tapestry that her mother, *nonna* Elsa, had embroidered, which portrayed a scene from one of the Medici's

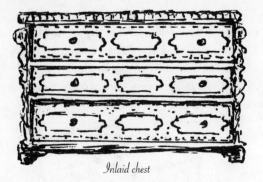

Inlaid chest

villas in Florence, copied, as she tells it, from a postcard. Next to the table was an antique inlaid chest, probably my favourite piece of furniture along with a Russian icon that vanished while in the process of being restored. All that remains is the frame with its passe-partout of dark red velvet and its gilt carved wood which now holds the icon of the Saints Cyprian and Justine, in memory of the monastery of the same name in Greece where Paolo and I were married. A modern lamp made out of a white opaque net-like material illuminated this area. This created a diffused lighting effect, which also gave the dining area the sought-after air of formality.

I can remember the first time we laid that dining table with the tablecloth from my mother's trousseau, white with small green and pink embroidery, for the first important meal I ever prepared – risotto with quail, accompanied by a 1964 Barolo, a superb vintage. I realised the value of those bottles of wine, bought to celebrate my birth, only when they were stolen. If I had been aware of how much they were worth, I would never have used them to marinate the hare *in salmi'* for a Christmas dinner.

QUAIL RISOTTO

8 quail
8 thin, wide slices *pancetta tesa*
1/2 glass brandy
meat stock
finely grated Parmigiano Reggiano

Since quail are tiny and consist mainly of bones, I allow two per person, and three for Giudi.

The quail (previously plucked and dressed by the butcher) are wrapped in the pancetta slices, browned at high heat for 2 minutes each side, then doused with the brandy, which is left to evaporate. Transfer the quail to a deep ovenproof dish with a lid and cook them in the oven at 180°C for 10 minutes, with 2 glasses of meat stock, preferably veal so as not to drown the delicate flavour. The pancetta is the secret to this recipe – it keeps the quail tender and tasty.

The risotto is cooked separately. It's a 'white' risotto, made with a good veal stock and *mantecato* at the very end with a knob of butter and finely grated Parmigiano Reggiano.

This is a meal in one: the quail with the pancetta removed are served on top of the risotto.

There was a second table in the corner of the room surrounded by cork-panelled walls. It was a square card table with round legs of steel framing the corners of the tabletop and covered with green baize. There was a bracket of the same dimensions as the tabletop under the table from which you could extract four trays complete with ashtrays that rotated on the end of the table legs. We used this table whenever we all ate together, for lunch or dinner.

The lunch table

This is the table where I studied for my final school exams and for some university papers. In those days I would sit in what was usually my father's seat, with my back to the modern walnut wall unit that housed the red lacquer telephone. I remember my father grasping the phone in his large thickset hands, in order to point out with great theatrics the cost of the latest bill from Italian Telecom. I faced the bookcase, also made out of walnut and in the same style as all the custom-made furniture, composed of four long shelves filled with books. All were bound with dark leather and shared the same peculiar feature – none of them displayed their title on the spine, so it was always necessary to pull them out completely to read it. They had come mainly from my mother's house. There were the white Propilei history encyclopaedias, and the *Riccardo Ricciardi* collection of Italian classics, like Dante, Carducci and Pascoli. And finally there were the books which reflected the wide-ranging and ever-changing passions of my eclectic father: books on hunting, fishing and sailing. The novels were not to be found here, but were in my parents' room in a bookcase of the same style, but in this instance narrow and reaching the ceiling. On the table sat a large round lamp with a modern brushed steel finish, whose light was hooded and diffused by a smaller disc covering the light bulbs, thus giving it the appearance of a UFO.

At lunch I sat on my father's left, Giudi on his right and our mother opposite him. Sometimes I would return home at 1.30 and find the table set here instead of in the kitchen. I knew then that my father would be joining us for lunch. Everything that had anything to do with the family – school holidays, requests or protestations – was discussed at the table when we sat down to eat, often downplayed by Giudi's sharp sense of humour. I remember with pleasure those winter lunches when returning home from school with a hearty appetite, I would slip on my warm fluffy slippers, truly one of life's small pleasures for

carciofo

those of us with chronically cold feet, and take my seat at the table. Lunch was simple, but was always varied, often consisting of three courses. Usually there was an *antipasto* of *pinzimonio*: slices of raw vegetables, always carrots and celery, fennel in winter and artichokes in spring, dipped in olive oil. My mother adored artichokes and bought them by the dozen, returning home from the market with the plastic bags perforated by the thorns. She put them in vases as if they were flowers with extremely long stems, which she believed to be tastier than the heads, and armed with infinite patience she cleaned them one by one,

finocchio

frequently emitting sharp squeals of pain when she encountered small thorns hidden beneath the internal leaves. These days the job of cleaning the artichokes falls to my sister, because our mother has the ready excuse that she doesn't see so well and can't work with her glasses on which, on the rare occasions she manages to find them, she insists on wearing precariously perched on her nose.

Preparing artichokes takes time, patience and preferably the use of gloves, because when you have finished your nails are black, just as your tongue would be if you ate them raw. Each time I buy them I wonder if I do so just because I like them and not because their preparation evokes childhood memories. Roman artichokes known as *mammole*, big and rotund and lacking thorns, were an exception, and were cooked *alla romana* the way they cook them in Rome.

CARCIOFI ALLA ROMANA

small bunch of parsley, chopped together with a clove of garlic
2 tablespoons breadcrumbs
salt and pepper
4 fresh artichokes
2 tablespoons olive oil

Mix together the parsley, garlic, breadcrumbs. Add a pinch of salt and pepper.

Trim the artichokes, discarding external woody leaves, and remove the fibrous, woody, bitter external part of the stalk. The heart of the stalk is lighter in colour and is easy to identify. Press the head of the artichoke down onto a work surface, so the leaves separate and open without becoming detached. Use your fingers to sprinkle the filling into them.

Arrange the artichokes, heads facing upwards, in a saucepan

containing 2cm of water, drizzle with olive oil and cook covered at low heat for 45 minutes, adding another 2cm of water if required. Place the artichokes on a serving platter together with the juices. If by any chance there are any left over, they are perfect for making a risotto, which should be finished off with Parmigiano Reggiano.

Following the *antipasto* came a first course, alternating at lunch and dinner, of pasta or rice with vegetables, or a second course of meat or fish. More than one *contorno* – a side dish of cooked or raw vegetables – was always on offer at both meals. This was usually salad, which my mother would serve in infinite varieties. Not just plain lettuce, but the pale green sweet *riccia*, the winter salads of *cicorie*, the round red *radicchio* from Chioggia, the multicoloured bitter red and white *spadone trevigiano*, the crunchy white *belga*. There were the spring salads of tender green *valerianella*, the tender and cheerful *lollo*, the tiny and piquant *rucola*. The salads were always bursting with colour and always had an indulgent touch of walnuts or cheese, such as flakes of Grana Padano, little pieces of *quartirolo* or sharp piquant radish. In spring, if we were in the mountains, there were wild chicory sprouts, which appear from the hedges in the last traces of muddy snow. In the *spadone trevigiano* country you would find dandelion, a veritable chemist's shop given its numerous nutritional and medicinal properties. Popularly known as 'dog tooth', it's bitter, but if used when it has just sprouted is perfect with hard-boiled eggs and new onions. It is a liver cleanser and a rich source of iron, perfect after rich winter foods.

The dressing was always the same, olive oil and vinegar for the salads and olive oil and lemon for the cooked vegetables, except for cauliflower, which is best dressed with vinegar.

My father's favourite dish, even though he didn't drink milk, was roast pork in milk, to which you add a few drops of lemon when it has almost finished cooking, causing the dish to thicken and giving it its distinctive taste.

LONZA DI MAIALE AL LATTE

60g butter
1 small onion, finely chopped
600g pork loin
250ml (1 cup) whole fresh milk
salt and pepper
juice of half lemon

Heat butter in a heavy saucepan and sweat the onion. Add the meat and brown it. When well browned, add the milk and season with salt.

Cover and continue cooking at very low heat for about an hour and a half, adding more milk if necessary.

At the end of cooking time the quantity of milk will be reduced and will be mixed with the meat juices, forming, small globules of curd similar to cottage cheese in appearance.

Remove the meat and place to rest for 10 minutes. In the meantime, add the lemon juice and a little freshly ground pepper to the pan brownings, stir over a low flame for 2 minutes and take off the heat.

Slice meat into thin slices and serve with sauce and some plain boiled spinach or *ripassati* (cooked spinach, tossed in a pan to flavour with some butter and a good tablespoon of grated Parmigiano Reggiano cheese). Alternatively, serve with a handful of silverbeet, boiled and dressed with olive oil, salt and the juice of one lemon.

I loved *frittata*, which my mother made, managing to transform each one into a new and unique dish, partly because she could never remember the exact ingredients she used each time. It is a great way of using up left-overs.

Cioccolatino was a favourite of Giudi's when she was little. It isn't a real recipe, more an improvised sweet, made when my mother felt like something indulgent. She mixed 4 tablespoons of softened butter, which is never salted in Italy, with cocoa, sugar and as much rum as personal taste dictated. This was left to cool in the fridge and then spread on bread.

In our house bread was the indisputable star of the table. My mother took great pleasure in trying different types of bread: *michetta, maggiolino, francesini,* but above all multigrain and wholemeal bread with pumpkin and sunflower seeds. *Ciabatta* only arrived in bakers' shops years later. My father would reproach my mother for eating too much bread, but she couldn't help herself. Bread had its roots deep in her childhood memories, when it was often eaten with butter, in the same way that fresh pasta evokes childhood memories for my father. Their cultural conditioning demonstrates how Italian cooking was until only recently more truly identifiable as regional cuisine.

Each of the twenty regions, which until the unification of Italy in 1851 were broken up and reassembled according to the economic and political interests of the various conquerors, has produced a cuisine which is strongly linked to locally available ingredients, and in the case of regions with ports or borders, shaped by external influences. The *crescentina* is a perfect example of this. Delicious strips of deep-fried pasta which inflate when they are thrown into boiling oil or lard, they are eaten with *coppa* or salami. In Bologna they are called *crescentina*, while in Modena only 30km away they are known as *gnocco fritto*, not to be confused with *gnocco* – a dumpling from Reggio Emilia which refers to a savoury cake containing *ciccioli*, pure fat in the form of pieces of pork crackling. And they should most definitely never be confused with *la gnocca*, which in colloquial Italian means a beautiful girl and is often followed by a wolf-whistle.

Only since the seventies has Italian cuisine shed its regional character in favour of a national identity. And despite having its roots in tradition, it is moving towards a new vision of cuisine which is about the choice of high quality ingredients in season and minimal cooking times in order to highlight flavours. This new culinary vision is also about combining the simplicity of Mediterranean cuisine, which is healthy and appetising, with creativity, without overlooking the importance of taste.

Behind where I sat at the table was the door made of walnut and covered with cork panelling which you passed through in order to gain access to the rest of the house. A long, narrow, windowless corridor was divided in two by a door that created a boundary between the living and sleeping areas. The first half of the corridor was completely covered by white-walled cupboards the height of the ceiling, which in this part of the house had not been lowered, with two doors that led to the kitchen. The interior of these doors was lacquered in bottle green to match the colours in the rest of the room. The kitchen was poorly lit, with terracotta tiles, modern furniture and the ever-present marble table, characteristic of Italian kitchens. The only window was a French door opening onto a small terrace always cluttered with empty sparkling-water bottles. Off this terrace was the heavy iron gate that also served as the service entrance and which we used most of the time.

It was at that table that we had our hurried breakfasts, barley and hot milk for the children, *caffé latte* – coffee with milk – for the adults, or just a short black for my father, and every now and then a few plain biscuits. Breakfast in this form is a dreadful habit we Italians still cling to and which as a consequence means we have huge appetites by lunchtime. Thank goodness for the interval at school for the morning play lunch and the office break for a cappuccino and a brioche.

The only time I can remember my father cooking it felt as though a great event was about to take place. He had done the grocery shopping himself but had asked my mother to help him in the kitchen. She was well aware of the consequences his cooking would have on the state of the kitchen and so had also enlisted our help.

The recipe was *faisan à la bohémienne*.

Who knows why it is that when men want to demonstrate their expertise in the kitchen they always choose French cuisine? The Cooking Institute where I attended evening courses on *haute* and international cuisine and where we learnt the most elaborate and pretentious recipes was frequented mainly by businessmen who, once they had divested themselves of their suit jackets, ties and mobile phone earpieces, were transformed into expert cooks. Driven by my curiosity, I undertook a small survey with the unsurprising result that men maintain that 'cooking' is a feminine prerogative and its purpose is survival – 'you cook to live' – whereas *haute cuisine* is an art form far removed from the requirements and necessities of everyday life. Sometimes I think that I chose a business career in order to be able to dedicate myself to cooking in its cultural and artistic form.

The preparation of ingredients alone took a good few hours and all the available bench space. My father bought a large apron for the occasion and it conferred on him the air of a true professional. Judging by his expression, he felt like a real chef.

The pheasant had been plucked and cleaned. The ingredients were *fois gras* flavoured with salt and paprika, *picchiettato* – dotted with little cubes of white truffle and then slowly cooked in a reduction of water and Madeira wine. *Pichiettare* is a proper cooking term, which means to make incisions in something using a specially designed utensil like a large needle, to insert traces of extraneous ingredients.

This process was the cause of the first argument. For my mother, cooking a truffle was already a sacrilege, never mind adding insult to injury with the waste incurred as a result of the subsequent operation. The *fois gras* was cooked and inserted in the bird, taking care not to rupture it, which was extremely difficult given its gelatinous consistency. But it didn't end there. The pheasant also had to be larded, another technical term the same as the first, with the only difference between them being that lard is inserted into the bird by means of the special utensil and then held fast by means of strips of bacon and kitchen twine. My grandmother must never have taught my father to sew. After long arguments and ruinous spillages of the precious stuffing, the poor bird was full of wounds and tears worthy of a commander returning from the war. The kitchen to all intents and purposes looked like a battlefield.

Once the pheasant had been cooked my father served it with all the pyrotechnic drama of the *flambé* by lighting the cognac that surrounded the bird. It did taste good, but we all agreed that the next time he felt like cooking we would go to a restaurant in Paris. It would be less exhausting and probably cheaper too.

My father's most successful culinary efforts came when he returned from the *gastronomia* or delicatessen, usually on Saturdays on the rare occasions we stayed in town. Those wonderful trays wrapped in thick silver paper and firmly held in place by ribbons are to this day my preferred alternative to dinner in a restaurant, even if they are sometimes more expensive. My father had his office in Via Turati, the street which goes from the huge central train station (a typical example of Fascist architecture), right up to Piazza Cavour and then beyond the perimeter of the city walls, passing through the two low arches in Via Manzoni right up to La Scala theatre and from there to the Duomo.

The famous *Salumeria* Principe, along with Salumaio in Via Monte Napoleone and Peck's, were recognised as the temples of gastronomy in Milan. I can vividly recall the window at Principe's, with its enormous platters full of ready-to-eat specialities, always incredibly fresh and beautifully presented. Whole lobster and salmon *in bellavista* were surrounded by piped decorations of sensual mayonnaise. Shrimps and bright red prawns seemed to still be swimming. Mushroom salads of funny *ovuli*, which always look dubious to me even if they are the favourites of mushroom

connoisseurs. Salads of large slices of raw *porcini*, perfectly
formed without the usual holes made by worms, and served with
slices of Parmigiano Reggiano.

I share with my father a love of cheese, especially for Gorgonzola. In the food speciality shops in Milan you will find it blended
with the locally produced *mascarpone* with the indulgent addition
of whole walnuts, which creates not just a unique flavour, but also
an unexpected contrast between the creamy and velvety smooth
consistency of the Gorgonzola and *mascarpone*, and the crunchy
and woody character of the walnuts.

One of the walls of the kitchen had a large opening allowing for
food and plates to be passed through from the informal dining
room which we hardly ever used. Initially serving as a laundry it
soon became the room of Mary, Giudi's beautiful nanny from the
Seychelles, and subsequently was used by Candida, the *au pair* who
lived with us for more than seven years and was like a sister to me.
Only four years older, she was from Madonna dei Monti, a small
village of few inhabitants near Santa Caterina di Valfurva in
Valtellina.

Candida lived with her parents and four brothers, all with
ruddy complexions and a particular smell I was able to identify
only much later. I remember entering her house one cold but
sunny winter's day. Outside the light was blinding due to the
reflection of the snow on the surrounding mountain peaks and the
interior was almost completely shrouded because there was

just one window. After the few seconds it took for my eyes to accustom themselves to the semi-darkness I saw her mother in front of the *stufa*, the cast-iron stove used for both heating the house and for cooking. She is preparing *polenta* and on the table covered with a plastic tablecloth sat a large, thick chopping board with *scimudin*, the local cheese, on it. The heat emanating from the stove found its way into the furthest corners of the room and in penetrating the adjacent living space manages also to heat the sleeping area. These were the only two rooms; there was no bathroom. Her parents slept in the room with the stove so they could add new wood to it as soon as they woke up; the children slept in the other room. The smell which always accompanied Candida was the smell of her house, of the *stufa* and of *polenta*.

Giudi and I slept in the same room with walls covered by an extremely glossy special washable material. The ceiling was hung with paper with huge multicoloured poppies on it, which made you feel as if you were inside a fairytale. Every morning when I woke in the semi-darkness and found myself surrounded by those stylised flowers I would let myself be transported by childhood dreams. Years later I wanted to paper the walls with sky blue wallpaper and the ceiling in dark blue. I didn't realise that I would have lost a little of that magic that only fairytale pictures can evoke.

The writing desk was placed near a wall and was long enough for the two of us to be able to sit comfortably at it. It was a really bright yellow, and the search for that exact shade of yellow haunts me to this day. It had a row of drawers on one side only and a cupboard on castors; we removed the castors and it subsequently became the surface of my children's dressing table. The beds were placed alongside the other two walls, with bedspreads in bright matching colours.

Our balcony overlooked the same small internal courtyard as our parents' room, with just the one large tree. The courtyard, however, was no good for playing in. It is a courtyard that evokes sad memories for me, all of them connected to sounds. We heard the first one when we had not been living there for long, a dull and sinister thud, which we later found out had been made by the body of an old man who lived on the top floor. The second one was my mother's yells as she surprised a thief in the process of stealing her bicycle. And the last one was the definitive howl of our dog Sock paying final homage to my father, who was taking his leave from us forever, in the next room.

It's funny, but I remember that I cooked that night and I can still taste the slightly metallic flavour of the tomato, sage and chilli salsa, or perhaps I simply remember the taste of the fear of being left abandoned.

Giudi, who was seven, had been sent to stay with friends in the days preceding my father's death. My mother and I never wept together; sorrow has no companions. I watched Candida as she busied herself organising the funeral arrangements. Sock simply vanished only to reappear the day after my father had died.

We wandered around the house in a dreamlike state, no tears, like ghosts at home on the earthly plane, attending to the many formalities that we had to deal with. On more than one occasion we had a chuckle at the thought of my father's reaction to the seemingly absurd choices and decisions we had to make.

Even though I thought I was psychologically prepared for his death, I now know that no one is ever ready to say that final goodbye to the people they love, the absence of their physical presence leaves a hole that no memory, no matter how strong, can ever fill.

I have always drawn strength from the memory of my father's love for us, his joy for life, his optimism and his faith, and while all these things have given me a real sense of security, I feel his absence most keenly in the happiest and most important moments in my life, where I would give anything to hear the sound of his voice and his resounding laugh.

The last room was accessed by descending three small wooden stairs and belonged to my parents. On Sunday mornings we woke my father by bringing him coffee in bed and it was the perfect moment for cuddles. My mother had designed their bed, a large king-size one, by placing two simple wooden bases side by side with their wire nets for the wool mattresses on eight thick antique bed legs shaped like a lion's paws. The headboard literally 'crowned' the bed. Of the same period as the legs, it was composed of a half-moon of sky-blue satin, the same as the bedspread, from which emanated 'rays' of gilded wood of different lengths, arranged in a semicircle.

As big as this bed was, once Sock arrived with his tail a-wag, we would find ourselves demoted to the floor. Sock was a German Shepherd. It's a funny name for such a big and solid dog but I chose it after reading Mickey Mouse comics. 'Sock' was the graphic image of the sound of someone throwing a punch. I had no idea what the word really meant in English. The sound matched a dog of his size and bearing, even though the word's real meaning suited him somewhat less. After Sock, my mother chose a cat, who despite being gigantic, didn't take up too much space.

GLOSSARY:

ANTIPASTO (ahn-teep-ah-sto) refers to small, appetising food portions served at the beginning of a meal. Plural: *antipasti*.

COPPA (kop-pah) is handcrafted using the muscles in the neck vertebrae of the pig. Unlike most sausages, the meat is not minced, but is simply salted and with herbs added, wrapped with intestine giving it a sausage-like appearance. Paolo's 90-year-old relative, who resides in the Oltrepo Pavese, still produces the best *coppa* I have ever tasted. His tip is that before slicing the *coppa*, you must soak it in red wine (a whole bottle); this makes it softer and tastier.

GORGONZOLA (gor-gon-tzo-la) DOP is blue cheese from cow's milk. Milk is pasteurised and heated to 30°C before inoculation with *Penicillium roqueforte* mould, milk enzymes and liquid calf's rennet. After 25–30 minutes, the soft curd is cut, first into three- to four-centimetre squares. These are allowed to stand in the whey for about ten minutes before they are cut more finely into walnut-sized lumps. After being bundled into thinly knotted cloths, they are drained for about half an hour. The firm curd is then transferred into perforated cylindrical moulds that are placed for about 24 hours on inclined boards, known as *spersori*, to encourage draining of the whey. Subsequently, the moulds are moved to the 'purgatories', or damp (96% humidity), warm (20–22°C) ripening rooms for four or five hours. They are then dry-salted. Today, high labour costs have induced some cheesemakers to use brine baths for salting instead. About one month later, the cheeses are perforated. This was once carried out with seasoned wood needles but nowadays steel or copper needles are inserted into the top and bottom of the cheese. The operation allows an even distribution of mould. 'Naturally fermented' Gorgonzola, also known as *del nonno* ('granddad's') or *antico* ('old-fashioned'), is produced in very limited quantities. It has much more conspicuous marbling, a crumblier body than normal and a much tangier flavour. The cheesemaking technique is similar, but some producers still leave the curd, which is precipitated in the evening, hanging from a stand overnight to drain and acquire the naturally occurring vein-producing mould present in the room. Another version, known as a *due paste* or 'two-curd', has today almost completely disappeared. It was made by leaving the curd from the evening milking overnight and pouring the milk onto it from the following morning's milking.

MANTECATO (mahn-teh-c-ahto) derives from the ancient Spanish word for butter. The term is used to define food preparations that have a creamy, glossy consistency.

MASCARPONE (ma-scar-po-ne) according to a colourful version originates from the Spanish expression *mas que bueno* ('more than good'), and dates back to the days of Spanish occupation. Mascarpone, or Mascherpone, is made from cream obtained by centrifuging or left to rise spontaneously. The fat content is variable, ranging from 25 to 40%. The cream is coagulated with organic acids by heating in a double boiler for about ten minutes at 85–90°C and stirring continuously. The curd is left to stand in the whey for 8–15 hours at a low temperature, then removed with cloths. After standing again for a short while, the remaining whey is removed and the Mascarpone is ready for the table. Excellent sprinkled with sugar and cocoa, Mascarpone is also used in the preparation of custards and desserts. It is thought to have came originally from the areas around Lodi and Abbiategrasso.

PANCETTA (pahn-cet-tah) is produced all over Italy where pigs are reared. It lines the ribs of the animal and is characterised by alternating streaks of fat and meat. The most common types are *tesa*, in slab form, aged for 20 days. In some regions of southern Italy, spices are added. There is also a smoked version, similar to English bacon; *coppata*, which is rolled around a piece of pork called *coppa* (see below); and *arrotolata*, the leaner cut of *pancetta* which is salted and peppered, then rolled up.

PINZIMONIO (peen-tzeem-onee-o) is a word comically created from the union of *pinᴢare* (literally 'to pinch, sting or nip as with tongs') and *matrimonio* for marriage.

QUARTIROLO (kwar-tee-rolo) DOP derives from the feed given to cattle during the cheesemaking period and refers to fresh grass fodder from the fourth cut, the *quartirolo*, which is richer in fragrance and flavour. Today it can be produced all year round, but the best *quartirolo* is still made in autumn, from early September to the end of October. *Quartirolo* contains whole or pan-skimmed cow's milk from two or more milkings. Coagulation takes place at around 35–40°C in 25 minutes. The curd is cut into hazelnut-size lumps in two stages that depend on the changing level of acidity in the whey. The curd and whey are then put into moulds and ripened at 26–28°C for 4–24 hours. Salting can be done dry or by soaking in brine. Soft *quartirolo* matures in 5–30 days. After 30 days' ageing, it can be labelled 'mature'. *Quartirolo di monte* is the version made in mountain dairies using milk fresh from the cow, and without added enzymes. It is ripened in a naturally warm, damp environment and dry-salted. The rind is thin and pinkish-white in the case of young cheeses and a reddish grey-green in the case of more mature cheeses. The body is compact and has small lumps. It is normal for small pieces to break away. Crumbly and soft, it acquires a melt-in-the-mouth texture as it ages.

SALMI' (sahl-mee) is a special cooking method used particularly for game, where the meat is left to marinate in wine, herbs and vegetables for a long time then is cooked very slowly together with the marinade.

SCIMUDIN (shee-moo-deen) is pasteurised cow's milk inoculated with a milk-based starter culture and heated to induce coagulation. The curd is broken up coarsely and poured into moulds, where it is left until the whey has drained off completely. Once dry, the firm curd is removed from the hoops, dry-salted and immersed in brine. It is then transferred to ripening rooms, where it is left at a temperature of 3–6°C in 85–90% humidity for a minimum of three or four weeks.

CHAPTER FOUR

Winters in Valtellina

I wear red most of the time. It puts me in a cheerful mood, gives me confidence and it reminds me of those crisp and sweet-smelling apples which we bought by the crate in Valtellina, my winter playground for more than ten years. A northern offshoot of the Lombard region, framed by the Orobie Alps in the south and the Rezie Alps in the north, Valtellina is the bed of the river Adda. It is a long, wide valley that stretches from Lake Como to the source of the river Adda in the Stelvio National Park. Valtellina is the main valley, but it opens into a myriad of lateral valleys that have been hollowed out by river tributaries. Climbing the roads of these valleys you reach the Spluga, Maloja, Bernina and Stelvio passes, to name only the most famous, where you are confronted by imposing peaks and spectacular glaciers.

Ever since I was too young to remember, my mother and father would spend a lot of time in the mountains – every weekend for my father, and the whole winter season for my mother and I and often *nonna* Tina as well. You leave Lake Lario at the altitude of Colico and take the road that winds gently upwards, following the course of the Adda, crossing Valtellina to Bormio and then continuing on to the border with Switzerland. During the eight years that we rented the house at Bormio for the winter season, we explored many of the lateral valleys, each of them surprisingly different. If I think back to the many excursions in search of new places, I realise that I can recall with ease the gastronomic specialities I tasted in each of them.

The road that leads to upper Valtellina passes through Sondrio, the main town. All I can remember of Sondrio, from those rare few occasions when we took the train, is the railway station. At the town gates, the small church of the Madonna della Sassella rises up on a rocky spur which dominates the vineyards, giving its name to one of the best known wines of the region – Sassella – a full-bodied red wine best suited to game, its ruby red hue bordering on the colour of garnets.

Even if wine was of no interest to me in those days, it was nonetheless entertaining to visit the *cantine* or cellars and discover the traditions of wine production handed down through the generations. There was always bread and salami, or bread and cheese, on hand – wine is best appreciated when accompanied by good food. I don't think I ever considered the existence of white wine, at least not until I began to drink it on my own. I liked the effect a drop of red wine made in a glass of water. The bright red colour of the wine fades as it mixes with the water in a slow spiral that eventually turns the water pink. The sound of mixing red wine with sparkling water – *acqua e vino* – belongs to my childhood as much as *caffé latte* does. The latter wasn't really coffee, but was usually barley or, on rare occasions, Ovolmaltina, sweet cocoa masquerading as a health drink. When it came to a good wine, my mother would prohibit me from diluting it with water. That barbarous act was reserved for wine that was called *da tavola* – table wine – though I'm not exactly sure why.

The vineyards that produce Grumello are found surrounding the 13th century castle of the De Piro family, built on a rocky hillock and dominating the lower part of the valley. The castle gives its name to the wine. With similar characteristics to Sassella, Grumello is a mature wine that goes perfectly with the cuisine of Valtellina.

Rich and full-bodied, Inferno is another wine best drunk when mature. Walking among the Inferno vines I discovered for myself how the name had come about. In a deep and precipitous valley, the vines are baked by the reflection of the sun on the rocks.

I have only recently discovered the less well known Sfursfat, a wine best suited to contemplation and conversation during those cold evenings with friends around the fireplace. It goes really well with local cheeses – I like white dessert wine with mature mountain cheeses.

Beyond Sondrio lies Teglio, a village almost unknown today but once important due to its strategic position on the spice route from the port of Venice to Northern Europe. It is situated on a plateau at an altitude of 700 metres and overhangs the lower Valtellina. Potential invaders would have had to climb the mountain overcoming a vertiginous incline, loaded with *armi e bagagli*, all their belongings, and under fire from the fortifications that towered over them. But far from being an isolated stronghold, Teglio was the centre of a dense communications network over which travelled leather goods, gold items, and pieces of machinery from Switzerland, Austria and Germany. Fine fabrics, salt, wine and flour came from the east and the south. So it is hardly surprising to find Palazzo Besta, an elegant, exquisitely frescoed mansion, unexpected in a mountain village whose oldest part dates back to AD 1300. It is said that the dynasty had its origins in England where the name 'Besta' – the best – comes from. The men of Besta are strong and courageous, but also men of some culture as the *palazzo* is one of the most elegant examples of Renaissance architecture. My favourite room is the *taverna*, with its walls of carved wood and its barrelled ceiling bordered by inlaid beams. In this room adjacent to the falconry, the nobles would gather after shooting parties to eat game and drink good wine. In an old letter you even find advice for treating hangovers. 'Eat bitter almonds and drink half a glass of cauliflower juice diluted by fresh water and wear a necklace with an amethyst pendant.' Try it and see.

The plateau enjoys a moderate climate which was well adapted to the cultivation of every type of crop and grain, with barley, grapevines, and forests of chestnuts and fir trees providing ample wood for the construction of dwellings, as well as for heating and cooking. There was also plenty of water, for fishing and for driving the water mills. But such good fortune eventually did run out, in this case in the 17th century with a massacre called *il Sacro Macello* – the Sacred Slaughter. A priest was murdered inside a church, and many men, women and children went to their deaths in an absurd struggle that was apparently about religion but really turned to economic and territorial interests.

Here the best buckwheat of the valley is produced – a humble ingredient that popular imagination has transformed into irresistible and flavoursome dishes. *Pizzoccheri*, coarse tagliatelle cooked with potatoes and *verza* (Savoy cabbage) and seasoned with butter, garlic and the local *bitto*, a typical alpine cheese, have become the most well known dish in the whole of Valtellina. Here, at the end of July, they hold the ancient Festival of the Pizzoccheri.

PIZZOCCHERI

300g buckwheat flour
100g white flour
200–250ml water
2 potatoes
1/2 Savoy cabbage
300g *bitto* or any good melting cheese
2 leaves fresh sage
100g butter
1 clove of garlic

Make dough with the two flours and water. Knead for about 10 minutes – I add some oil to aid elasticity, but I never tell anyone – then wrap dough in clingfilm and leave to rest for half an hour. Using a rolling pin, roll dough out until a 1cm sheet is obtained. Cut into 'tagliatelle' strips, 5cm long by 1cm wide.

Cut peeled potatoes into small pieces and slice cabbage into good-sized strips. Place potatoes and cabbage into a large pot of boiling salted water. After 5 minutes have passed, add the *pizzoccheri* and cook for a further 10 minutes. Drain all together, transfer to a large bowl and layer with cubed cheese. Heat butter in a pan and sauté garlic until golden, then pour over *pizzoccheri*.

A positively rich, wholesome and scrumptious dish.

Another speciality made from buckwheat is *polenta taragna*, which uses a more finely ground flour and is seasoned with butter and full fat cheese.

Tirano was a compulsory stop for buying milk on the journey to Bormio, and we always stopped at the same *latteria.*[1] Even if I

---

1   A small shop specialising in dairy products like milk and cheese.

had fallen asleep, I always woke up at this point. In the months of September and October the orchards in the fields that bordered the road were a blaze of red from the endless rows of apples. From early morning until dark you could buy crates of freshly picked fruit that were usually finished before we returned home at the end of the weekend.

Only a kilometre from the Swiss border is the terminus for the 'little red train of Bernina', which once ran on cogwheels and takes a spectacular route, trudging slowly to the Bernina Pass then on to St Moritz, the world-famous ski resort for the rich and famous in the upper Engadina. Tirano's specialities include *chiscioi*, a local focaccia always made with buckwheat and topped with aged cheese, and *grappa* which is produced in abundance and distributed in the streets during the festival of the same name held at the end of August.

grappa distiller

For the remainder of the journey my face would be glued to the window. It was pretty unlikely that there would be snow even in winter because the entire road passes through the bottom of the valley at an altitude of 400–500 metres above sea level, always flanking the river Adda on one bank or the other. Then there is a wide bend and a hill, at the foot of which appears unexpectedly the Sanatorium of Sondalo, once a treatment centre for the delicate illness of consumption because of its sunny position 900 metres above sea level and its dry and mild climate.

With a reputation dating back to the ancient Romans, because of the thermal baths still in use today at the majestic complex of the Bagni Vecchi, Bormio is a well-equipped ski resort in upper Valtellina on the edges of the Stelvio National Park. The town winds along Via Roma, the main street, until you reach the oldest part of the city centre, Piazza del Kuerc – which means lid or cover in local dialect – and here you find an old *loggia*[2] with a slate roof around which the citizens would gather for public meetings. The municipal tower is also located in the square with the Baiona, a huge bell which rings to summons the city council and to celebrate I Pasquali, a popular ancient festival during which the five original town districts (called *reparti*) parade, each of them carrying their own *pasquale*, a float made according to a design that remains secret right up to the day of the procession. Each district is represented by a shepherd boy carrying a lamb (Easter in Italy is in spring when the animals give birth to their young), so that it can be blessed in the local church. For the occasion all the inhabitants wear traditional dress, the men in black cloth breeches, long white woollen socks, a red sash around their waists, a white shirt with a brightly coloured neckerchief and a large-brimmed black cloth hat. The women wear full red cloth skirts, white shirts and wide black or brightly coloured scarves.

This pastoral festival recalls the benediction of the flocks, the only source of sustenance, before they were moved to the summer mountain pastures.

The first place we rented in Bormio was an apartment on the top floor of a small modern building on the outer edges of town. The owners of the *building* also ran a *pizzeria* called La Stua, another compulsory stop before we returned home at the end of the weekend. On the other side of the road from the *pizzeria* there was a cheese factory where we were able to stock up on the local cheeses, among which was my favourite, *scimudin*, with its creamy consistency and mild flavour.

---

2   A typical feature of Italian urban architecture of the Medieval/Renaissance period – a type of large covered veranda or open gallery.

Behind the house was a hedge with a henhouse and behind that the Frodolfo stream, whose source is the Forni glacier and which further south flows into the Adda. On the rare occasions when we would spend a weekend here at the end of summer, I liked to explore the length of the stream, jumping from rock to rock with a tape recorder slung over my shoulder so I could listen to music (this was before the advent of the Walkman). There is the distinctive sound to mountain streams and the smell of fresh mountain air accompanies their flow. In a few places the clear water makes its way slowly between boulders that have been dried by the sun, making them safe to walk on. The air was gentle and it was pleasant to sit and admire the surrounding mountains, still green despite the summer months. In other places the water flows quickly, bubbling and gurgling, the air is sharper and it is necessary to think twice about where you put your feet. I nearly always returned home drenched, though I would stop briefly to greet the chickens and to check whether they had laid any eggs.

Although I hated leaving at dawn, I knew that you only find mushrooms while it is still dark, but ever since the day I stumbled upon a *porcino* at lunchtime, I am convinced that it is possible to savour the joys of life at a more respectable hour.

Anyway, if it was the season, my mother would organise walks in the forest in search of the *porcini* mushrooms that grow in abundance in the nearby Valdidentro. At Oga on one of these enforced expeditions, at the end of a long morning's search which had not been terribly successful, I was walking through the forest whose density allowed for only the smallest amount of light. I realised only just in time that I was about to step on an enormous mushroom. Convinced that it was poisonous, and annoyed because it was obstructing the already laborious slope, I was on the point of treading it underfoot when my mother's yells prevented me from committing an unparalleled gastronomic crime. It was a huge *porcino*, surrounded by a family of smaller *porcini*. Once home, I wanted to clean it myself. I carefully removed the earth and detached the stalk in order to cook it with the other mushrooms, also *porcini* but less perfect as small wormholes were visible. I cut the cap into thick slices and my mother seasoned it with a dressing of oil, parsley and a sprinkling of shaved Parmi- 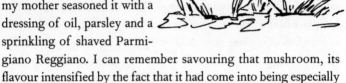 giano Reggiano. I can remember savouring that mushroom, its flavour intensified by the fact that it had come into being especially for me, at the same time reinforcing the absurdity of a dawn rising.

The forests also bring another taste to mind, the taste of fear at being lost.

In those days at Oga there was a ski establishment and one icy cold winter's day when there had not been much snowfall, my mother and father had decided to have lunch in the alpine hut. It was a typical meal of *polenta taragna* with chamois stew and *porcini* mushrooms; having no one to play with, I had asked for and been granted permission to go skiing on my own. The descent into the dense forest seemed interesting but after a series of crossroads and deviations I realised I was lost. I couldn't even ski very fast because there were so many bald spots without snow. By now I was some distance away from the ski lift and I couldn't recall having seen anyone. So I removed my skis and began my descent on foot, hoping to come across some adult. I don't know how long I kept walking but I became really scared and soon enough began to cry. The silence of the forests in winter is complete, and the light that is minimal under normal circumstances becomes even fainter on cloudy days.

With all those detours I had made, how on earth would they be able to find me? My nose felt as if it was about to drop off from the cold, my hands and feet were frozen, and I couldn't decide whether to keep descending or whether to try and go back up. At last I heard the familiar sound of skis on snow and found myself face to face with a boy whom my mother would later describe as charming – but I was only little, and I had my mind on other matters. I was in tears and had absolutely no desire to zip about on my skis in search of snow, so my saviour decided that the quickest solution was to piggyback me on his shoulders. I can't have been gone all that long as my mother and father didn't seem particularly worried when I made my entrance into the warm hut. My father downplayed the whole episode, while my mother bombarded me with hugs and kisses, a tactic which later became increasingly less successful, given my attempts to avoid the vigorous outbursts of affection that she always employed to express her love.

I was still shivering, more from fright than cold, so my mother made me a nice *vov*. This was the first recipe I ever commited to paper, obtained from the elderly proprietor of the alpine hut, and copied into the only notebook of recipes I have ever kept. Today, thirty years later, I am moved to see the yellowed pages and it gives me great pleasure to think that my daughters will make *vov* with the same recipe.

VOV

It is crucial that the 6 egg yolks used here and whisked together with 300g of sugar until white and frothy are as fresh as possible. Bring half a litre of milk to the boil together with the peel of one lemon and a further 200g of sugar – bear in mind that this is a tonic against the cold and is not a dietary drink. When the milk is cool, discard the lemon peel and very gradually add the well beaten egg yolks. At this point, add 100ml of Marsala and 100ml of pure alcohol. Pass through a fine sieve and bottle in 'long neck' bottles – which is what the recipe literally says – cork and leave to rest for at least 3 days.

At the bottom of the page there is a note where I specify that the recipe can use another ingredient, the eggshells. If left to steep in the alcohol they dissolve, further benefiting the drink by the addition of some precious calcium.

The main purpose for a side trip to Livigno was its status as a *zona franca*, a duty-free zone, exempt from *iva*[3] and customs tariffs. Many things cost significantly less there, starting with petrol. The customs concessions were the result of the enforced isolation of the town at one time which interrupted all means of communication for seven or eight months a year at almost 2000 metres above sea level. You can transport outside the duty-free zone a certain amount of tobacco, liquor, coffee and perfume; until just a few years ago there were also considerable savings on the purchase

---

3   Italian GST or VAT.

Braulio is the typical liqueur of High Valtellina made with a secret recipe.

of cameras, watches and articles of clothing. There were customs checks, however, and on one occasion my mother experienced at first hand just how little sense of humour the customs officers had. We had returned from one of these consumer raids with nothing more than a few packets of cigarettes and lots of chocolate and my mother jokingly responded to the demand of 'Anything to declare?' by saying that her husband with that innocent look of his could have easily smuggled drugs and still passed through customs undetected. The outcome was two hours during which the car, passengers and personal items were scrupulously examined. My father was silent for two days afterwards.

Beyond Valdidentro, the road rises again until it reaches Trepalle, which is the highest municipality in Europe at 2250 metres above sea level. At the Eira Pass you start to descend by means of a wide curving road towards the broad valley of the village made up of a single row of houses that stretches for 12km. Livigno is surrounded by two chains of mountains that gently slope from 3000 metres to the outer reaches of the village. The continual winter isolation, now overcome by the use of modern snow removal machines, has enabled the ancient pastoral traditions and mountain architecture to remain intact. The best time to appreciate these are during the month of December.

In a fairytale landscape completely covered in pure white snow, adorned with lights and Christmas decorations, you can see the silhouettes of the alpine huts and brick houses, most of them just two-storeyed and decorated with discreetly painted floral motifs and fretwork balconies. These are common the length of the alpine ranges of Europe and have been built according to an ancient design. You often notice a little peephole beside the front door, which according to ancient popular belief was a means for the householder's soul to ascend to heaven if the door was shut.

In one of these alpine huts, steeped in the bitter smell of rancid milk, we saw butter being made. I don't remember the man's face, only the odour that clung to him of grass, milk and pipe smoke. He let us taste the cream that is pure white in colour, even whiter than the milk and covered with a multitude of tiny bubbles that make it seem light. From the aluminium barrel in the odd shape of a large jam jar, the cream is poured neatly through a little hinged flap that opens into a small wooden barrel. Then by turning a worn handle, the barrel begins to spin. As well as the creak of the handle you hear the sound of the cream, which is at first a rustle of liquid that flows around the sides and then a dull thud as it thickens when it hits the bottom. After a few final energetic turns of the handle a bright yellow butter with a strong taste 'of cow', as my mother would say, emerges mixed with a greasy liquid.

I skied to the point of exhaustion on the ski slopes of Bormio. For some years I was also subjected to the torture of athletic training for the races that are a perfect schooling in discipline and team building. When training was over we would take shelter in the alpine huts for lunch.

A simple lunch at La Rocca alpine hut might consist of the local rye bread called *braʒadella*, the dialect word for *braccio* or arm. This was a hoop of bread made out of buckwheat and served at the table threaded over one arm, while the other was used to serve the wine. The *braʒadella* would be generously filled with *bresaola*. Then there was the more elaborate lunch on offer at the Chalet dei Rododendri, which would be a trio of first courses composed of

braʒadella

piʒʒoccheri, *sciatt* and *malfatti*, small gnocchi of flour, spinach, eggs, breadcrumbs and parsley seasoned with melted butter and sage.

SCIATT

150g buckwheat flour
100g white flour
salt
200ml water
150g cheese – any good melting cheese, like Fontina
1 tablespoon breadcrumbs
1 tablespoon *grappa* (optional)
1 teaspoon granulated dry yeast

Mix the two flours, add some salt, then add water to make a smooth but not too liquid batter. Add the cheese (cut into ¹/₂ cm cubes), breadcrumbs, and *grappa* if desired, then mix together. Add yeast, then leave to rest for 20 minutes. Use a tablespoon to scoop up batter containing cheese cubes and drop into hot oil. Fry until golden, drain on absorbent paper, and serve. (Sciatt literally means frog.)

When my father, exasperated by the long journey and above all with the persistent shortage of snow, chose Cervinia in Val D'Aosta instead, I was devastated. He responded by saying that we would go back to Valtellina when the motorway had been completed, in other words in four years' time. Four years, an age away! Looking back now, I don't know whether to laugh or cry at my reaction. I can still remember the last time I came down the Ciuck slopes. It was spring and there was so little snow that it made for a hazardous descent. But at that age who cares? In this season Bormio isn't very pretty. Only a few patches of muddy snow remain on the hedges and the sound of water becomes a constant backdrop. It is the sound of snow melting and running along the gutters and then into the drains. Rivulets run through the hedges then in their downward courses unite and create streams that are silent to begin with but bit by bit, as they get bigger, produce more noise. All this adds to the sound of the river that has descended from the melting glaciers, creating a harmonious and sweet-smelling refrain. The smell of the mountains in this season is unique, mixed as it is with that of the mud, damp grass, primroses, and in Bormio the scent of the larch trees still oozing melted snow.

My tears in that last and solitary descent were salty and inconsolable. To remind me of those years I still keep a *pezzotto*, a patchwork mat characteristic of the valley. Once the *pezzotti* were made by the women of the mountains by recycling old sheets and a collection of clothes and rags, which were then made into tiny strips to be woven together by a web of cotton thread. It is in a sorry state today and the colours have faded but I can't bring myself to throw it out.

GLOSSARY:

GRAPPA (grahp-pa) is pungent colourless brandy with an alcoholic content of about 40%, distilled from the pressed skins and pips of the grapes left after wine-making. At its crudest, *grappa* tastes of raw spirit, but after maturing the taste becomes refined. On the whole, you get what you pay for; cheap *grappa* is fiery and pungent, while expensive, well-matured varieties can be very smooth. The best *grappa* often comes in exquisite hand-blown bottles. The spirit can be flavoured with various aromatics, including rose petals and lemon peel.

CHAPTER FIVE

The seven sisters

I could no longer remember why I enjoyed eating apple pips so much when I realised that my mother was teaching my daughters to do the same thing. This strange family custom has been partly responsible for the development of my taste-buds. You can tell if an apple is any good from its pips. If they taste of almond and are sweet, the apple will be a good one. It is common for a taste to evoke a memory, but it is also a spontaneous reaction to associate one flavour with another.

My mother for example maintains that the best lobster should taste of almond. This is not as silly as it sounds. The complex arrangement of our taste-buds attests to the fact that the act of tasting can be broken down into distinct and successive moments, if only you take the time. And my mother is a master when it comes to taking the necessary time to *gustare*[1]. But then there is also the

---

1   *Gustare* in Italian is not just to taste, but to taste using all one's senses; to enjoy, to savour, to relish, to appreciate.

fact that she most certainly does have a special relationship with lobster, because it always features in the stories she tells of the most important moments in her life.

Once in Venice after a romantic and long – too long, according to my father – lunch of lobster, my mother fainted on the *vaporetto*[2] because the cold had blocked her digestion. And another time, again because of a lobster, she missed the ferry from Milazzo to Vulcano in the Aeolian Islands of Sicily, where I was waiting for her. I was ten, and my cousin Daniela had invited us to spend the summer in her beautiful house on the island of Vulcano.

The seven Aeolian Islands, volcanic and still active, are found in a strait not far off the northern coast of Sicily in the Tirrhenean sea. There names are Lipari, Vulcano, Salina, Stromboli, Panarea, Filicudi and Alicudi. You could describe each one simply by their colours.

The blinding white of the pumice stone quarries of Lipari, the largest of the islands, confers the sea with a splendour and transparency, which will always remain a strong memory for me. I relive in slow motion the feeling of that first dive from the small wooden fishing boat, when only a second earlier the white sea floor and the transparent water created the illusion of there being no water. And then, a moment later, once I have opened my eyes underwater I feel like I am being tossed in the air. When I resurface the intensity of the sun hitting the water reflects my almost motionless shadow on the blindingly white sea floor.

Then there is the rotten yellowy-green of the sulphur and the black volcanic ash of the island of Vulcano, which is the nearest to the coast. Salina, with its plentiful springs, was already known in Roman times as *la verde* – the lush island, for its abundant vegetation. Olive and citrus trees, grapevines and caper bushes and more than 400 different kinds of plants, half of which are found only on this island, reach as far as the volcanic crater which has been extinct for a long time.

---

2 Small steam-powered launch.

Stromboli has two colours, dark grey during the day and bright red at night, a result of the continual volcanic activity which hurls molten debris onto the slopes of the Sciara del Fuoco, the steep black lahar where the lava and debris flow down to the sea and solidify on contact with the water, a process accompanied by sizzling clouds of whitish vapour.

Panarea is the smallest of the islands at only just 3km long; it is the yellow of gorse and the red of ripe *fichi d'India*.[3] A tiny archipelago nestled among the larger archipelago of the other Aeolian Islands, it is surrounded by even smaller islands and reefs. Panarea is also the oldest island of the group, the first formed by the huge explosion of that underwater volcanic mass which gave rise to the seven sisters. Panarea is steeped in history and an interesting place from an archaeological perspective, full of prehistoric artefacts, and important enough to have been given its own historical classification, *cultura Capo Milazzese*, named after Cape Milazzo, the area in where the remains of a village inhabited in 1400 BC are found.

---

3 Prickly pears.

The waters of Filicudi are a colour which changes from blue to emerald green and then turn all the colours of the rainbow inside the Grotto of the Sea-ox, once a refuge for the now extinct monk seal. Alicudi, the furthest away, is the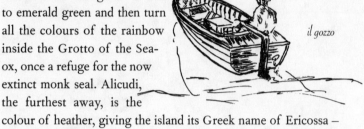

il gozzo

colour of heather, giving the island its Greek name of Ericossa – the Italian word for heather. When I visited it, just a few fishermen lived there, and my mother described it as 'the kingdom of silence'.

From the point of disembarkation on the beach we ascended a walkway with steps almost completely covered by caper bushes, in the direction of the few white houses on the upper plateau of the island whose view is lost in the surrounding endless expanse of blue. We came across two men, cloaked in that light which dissolves colours and blurs outlines. My father recognised the nets they had in their hands, large bow nets for catching the lobster that are abundant in these deep and rocky waters. My mother, who only needs to hear the word lobster, before she starts to swoon, asked if she could buy one. One of the men, wearing a characteristic Sicilian peaked cap called a *coppola*, replied that if we liked, his wife could cook some for us.

In the islands, man's relationship with the sea is still associated with survival and a profound respect for the forces of nature. My father explained this to me while the fisherman's silent wife immersed the still living creatures in boiling water. The only thing that could be seen emerging from the pot was their shells which, having turned blue, moved more slowly as time passed. My father explained that the screeching we could hear came from the air the creatures' carapaces emitted and wasn't the cries of animals in agony. My mother ran outside with Giudi in her arms with the excuse of gathering wild herbs to add to the salad. She ate lobster,

Giudi and Mum wearing a pair of her famous sumglasses.

but after her traumatic experience – as she describes it – at Mrs Kent's house on Jersey, she couldn't cook them.

She was fifteen and spent the summers in England, France or Germany in order to perfect her grasp of the languages she was studying at the Manzoni Linguistic Institute in Milan. According to my mother, Mrs Kent must have spent the whole day doing nothing except cook, because everything she remembers about that summer is associated with food: breakfast with elaborate cakes, the inevitable ritual of afternoon tea at five o'clock, with biscuits with coloured icing, and that lobster which had inadvertently escaped from her grasp, alarmed by the sound of boiling water. My mother ran into the kitchen just in time to see Mrs Kent pursuing the poor lobster and throwing it savagely into the boiling water where it had screamed in terror.

My mother is clearly a tragedian *manqué*. I was neither surprised nor horrified. I understood as children instinctively do that cooking the lobsters was neither a luxury nor an atrocity for that family, but instead a just reward for the fisherman's hard labour.

Whenever I try something new, even now, instead of being surprised or shocked by it, I do all I can to learn about the dish, which is after all a manifestation of the traditions and the culture that have created it. Often I discover the dish's origins have a religious significance or a subsistence role, and successive research brings to light its higher, aesthetic quality – best summarised in the word *raffinato*, meaning educated or cultured. I compare it with my taste experiences to date, I observe its external characteristics, its colour and consistency, I evaluate its freshness if necessary, then I try to break down the flavours in search of something I recognise. For me, such experiences have an important power to recall the past, as well teaching me as my father did in that kitchen in Alicudi, a profound respect for my fellow man.

Fully equipped with luggage, my mother, *nonna* Tina, my sister Giudi nearly three, and Mary our nanny, left to go on this exotic holiday as soon as school ended in June. My father was to join us at the end of August. Hardly off the plane we were struck by the blinding sun and suffocating heat, made even more unbearable by the air which instead of providing relief was like a warm blast from a hairdryer.

The air in Sicily is not characterised by any particular smell or fragrance; everything has been destroyed by the heat and intense brightness. Instead it is the evenings and the nights that reserve surprises for those of us guided by our sense of smell. In spring, the breeze that rises at sunset carries the scent of caper bushes in flower, of orange and almond trees. These fragrances accompany me in all my successive trips to Sicily.

We travel from Messina to Milazzo on a bus with no air conditioning. The hydrofoil doesn't have air conditioning either and it goes without saying that it doesn't leave on time. In any case we arrive at the island of Vulcano unscathed. We have remained inside the hydrofoil for the crossing so when we disembark we are unprepared for the strong smell of sulphur that hits us, and

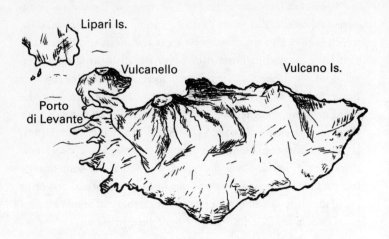

for a few moments it seems as if we have difficulty breathing. Mythology gives us an explanation for the phenomenon. Vulcan the blacksmith of Olympus had his workshops on the island, where his helpers, the Cyclops, manufactured lightning bolts for Jupiter, the King of the gods.

We berth in the port of Levante where the waters bubble as a result of the gases that are expelled from the underwater fumaroles. There we found a pool of grey mud, disgusting in my opinion, but wonderful and with health-giving properties according to my mother, so of course we had to go there more often than I wished to. When my father arrived, well aware of the risk he was running in being made to participate in that sticky and smelly bath, we discovered a bar close to the mud pool that served fantastic brioche with *granita*, which is a Sicilian speciality and a ritual that is played out at breakfast time for the whole of the endless summer. Brioches are round and flat in shape with a small hump on the top. On removing the hump you find that you have created a convenient hole that you can fill with *granita*. *Granita*, finely crushed ice, was originally lemon flavoured, but thirty years ago, as tradition would have it, Ernesto, a *pasticceria* from Catania, was responsible for greatly expanding the range of flavours. Coffee *granita* is a delight, especially at breakfast time, but not for the children who are allowed instead strawberry, lemon or almond *granita*, or my personal favourite which was mulberry-flavoured.

The berries are left to steep for a whole day in water and sugar. The infusion that is produced is then mixed with lemon juice and a pinch of vanilla and is served as a base for the beautifully scented *granita*.

The island is made up of two volcanoes, Vulcano and Vulcanello. Vulcano, the main island, was formed about 100,000 years ago and in the course of its numerous eruptions has often caused changes in the topography of the island. According to the testimony of Pliny the historian, in the first century BC an impressive underwater eruption was responsible for the emergence of Vulcanello, which around AD 1500 became part of the main island by means of an isthmus which separates the small bays of Ponente and Levante.

Daniela's house was near the summit of Vulcanello, a typical example of Aeolian architecture, with a white exterior and a flat roof for gathering the rainwater. The roof was ever so slightly slanted, which enabled the water to be channelled into terracotta drainpipes where it was kept in tanks built into the roof. From the gate, the whole house was hidden by a dense row of cluster pines; the strong smell of resin which they exuded proving so pungent as to be nauseating and responsible from that point on for my absolute avoidance of pine-needle bubble bath.

But perhaps another factor that contributed to this aversion of mine was because of a mischievous playmate who convinced me to try what she said was sweet pine nectar, when it was really pine resin. I can't remember her name, but I can picture her easily, short and plump, just as I was then, but her father believed that women should be curvaceous like Marilyn Monroe. While it gave me hope then, it proved to be a source of frustration later when I stood in front of the mirror as a teenager. And I can remember her house, which was even closer to the volcano's crater and for long periods could often remain cloaked in the vapour emissions that appeared from time to time.

One day at the end of summer, when the sun was not as high on the horizon and you were finally able to see even with the dazzling light, Daniela's parents led us into the Valle dei Mostri – the valley of the monsters, a stretch of black sand against which huge lumps of solidified lava had formed themselves into incredible shapes, funny rather than scary, and were silhouetted against the sky. On the return journey as the rules of good Sicilian hospitality dictate, they offered us a speciality of the Aeolian Islands, *i giggi*. These are a typical Carnevale sweet. Few other recipes can claim to be as widespread as the sweets prepared for Carnevale, with all their regional variations: *chiacchiere* in Milan, *crostoli* in the Veneto, *struffoli* in Naples and *frappe* in Rome. Even though they are all different shapes, they are made out of a simple dough of flour and water, with or without egg, and with flavours such as lemon, fried and covered with icing sugar. An essential ingredient of *i giggi* is *vin cotto*. This is also found in many different parts of Italy with infinite variations. As a rule, *vin cotto* is made with freshly pressed grape must and quince apples or dried figs are added to it. For my own personal variation I lightly simmer 2 bottles of good full-bodied red wine with 100g of honey, 200g of sugar, 2 cloves, a stick of vanilla and star anise. Simmer until the wine turns to syrup and you are left with around a half litre of it. I keep this preparation for the whole winter and I also use it in measures of half a glass to half a kilo of flour to add a nice flavour to the plainest biscuits.

GIGGI FROM THE AEOLIAN ISLANDS

500g plain flour
1/2 glass extra virgin olive oil
20g sugar
1/2 glass of Marsala (or sweet dessert wine such as Vin Santo)
1 teaspoon salt
1 egg yolk and 2 whole eggs
1 glass *vin cotto*
icing sugar
oil for frying

Mix together the flour, oil, sugar, egg yolk, whole eggs, Marsala and salt. Knead until a smooth ball of dough is formed. Place dough in a warm place to rest for a least an hour. Divide into fist-size portions and roll out into long sticks. Cut into 3cm pieces and fry in hot oil, then drain on kitchen paper.

Place the *vin cotto* in a saucepan and bring to the boil. Lower the fried *giggi* into the saucepan and stir for a minute or two until they have absorbed a good amount of wine. Lift them out using a slotted spoon. Dust with icing sugar. They keep for a week.

Once I created a non-alcoholic *vin cotto* recipe for a children's Carnevale party using the juice from syruped stoned cherries instead of wine. The flavour is less intense, but it keeps the mums happy.

My cousin's house was large, with a succession of rooms one after the other, whose French doors opened out onto a patio that smelt of bougainvillea and jasmine. In front of the patio there were comfortable and roomy wicker armchairs with huge round backs in the shape of seashells that enveloped you. I remember the lawn as being incredibly green on our arrival in June and scorched

Nonna Tina on the patio.

yellow by the time we left at the end of summer, when the pro-
longed dry weather would have caused some not inconsiderable
amount of damage with frequent fires and inconvenience due to
the water shortage. It was common until quite recently on some of
the islands, or during particularly dry summers even today, for
water to be transported to dwellings by tanker trucks that were
regularly replenished by tanker ships coming from Sicily.

In the middle of the lawn there was a swimming pool, thank
goodness, because the road that led to the sea was long and dusty,
unpassable in the summer heat between 11 a.m. and 5 p.m. at this
latitude. I didn't drive then and my mother is a lizard, capable of
lying under the scorching African sun for hours without moving.
By contrast, I have an exaggerated liking for water; she most
definitely has a closer relationship with wine. She has always said
that if water were wine she would have been an Olympic swim-

mer. With the passage of time, I begin to find some similarities between my mother and myself and, who knows why, to also better accept her defects. Though her overriding passion for good food can hardly be called a defect.

As soon as we arrived, we set off in search of places where we could try the local specialities and do the grocery shopping. Back then, the island wasn't as much of a tourist trap as it is now. The only big hotel had been closed for hygiene reasons – an invasion of mice! But in recompense, the fishermen sold fresh fish every morning, while the hydrofoil brought slices of broadbill taken from the straits of Messina. One of the recipes that I learned then and which follows me wherever I go is *Pesce spada 'a sfinciuni'*.[4]

SWORDFISH SFINCIUNI STYLE

6 swordfish (broadbill) steaks
oil, salt and pepper
dried oregano
2 onions cut into thin 'rings'
500g fresh ripe tomatoes
200g fresh breadcrumbs

Dunk broadbill steaks into a basting mixture made with a good helping of oil, salt, pepper and oregano.

Cover the steaks with onion 'rings' and slices of fresh tomato, then crumb steaks by pressing firmly, ensuring that the breadcrumbs stick well. Place steaks into a lightly oiled ovenproof dish, drizzle with oil and sprinkle with oregano, then bake at 180°C for 15–20 minutes.

---

4 *Sfinciuni* comes from *sfinciunaro*, a Sicilian dialect term referring to street vendors who sold a type of pizza with a thick base seasoned with tomato, onion and oregano – the ingredients used in this recipe.

Dad and the big volcano.

From the opposite side of the house, beyond the swimming pool a
balustrade borders the flat surface, creating a natural terrace under
which the steep part of Vulcanello slopes towards the sea. From
there you can see both the bays of the island and right in front,
silhouetted against a sky of cobalt blue, is the outline of the slopes
of Vulcano, rocky and dark, almost completely devoid of vegetation. As you walk beside the balustrade away from the house, a
small path leads to an incredible discovery which left me speechless
the first time I saw it: a tiny grotto, the height of a man, with an
opening that was big enough to enable the light to penetrate it
fully, full of rock crystals and sulphur in every conceivable colour,
made even more vibrant by the sunset that is the most spectacular
moment of the day in Sicily. The sky was still blue then, but the
sun was now low on the horizon and appeared enormous, such an
intense red that it seemed unable to withstand its own heat, and on
the point of immersing itself in the sea, almost as if seeking relief.
It was the same every evening; like a lovers' meeting, a serenade

which concludes with an embrace, suddenly the sun would dive into the sea and set it alight, colouring the water with hues from violet to gold and surrendering its fire.

My mother brought home some of the rocks from the grotto, a violet one, and a pink one. Even though so many years have gone by, when I look at those rock crystals I can still feel the emotions of that Aeolian sunset.

After sunset, which is late in summer, it's time to get dinner ready. In Sicily work resumes at 4 p.m. after the break for lunch. The kitchen was in the smallest part of the house and dinner was served on the wooden table in the covered patio in front of the kitchen, on the edge of the lawn that you reached by means of three steps. There were always guests, but not always ones we had invited. As darkness fell a small fleet of tiny flying insects would descend on us. They were so persistent that after a few days we surrendered to them, and for the whole of the summer we learned to cohabit with one small concession – we would remove them from each mouthful before we ate.

Another unwanted guest was a small and agreeable mouse who terrorised my mother. She has never been wild about 'small animals' and conceding to share her meal had already been a test of courage. A mouse was really beyond her. But it's not that easy to get rid of a rodent – first you have to flush it out. My mother practised non-violence towards animals and so she decided to let it live, feeding it every night with a small piece of cheese a good distance away from her room. I on the other hand had to contend with a visit from a huge salamander that had been attracted to my room by the light. In the end my mother and I both decided to roam the house with just the moonlight to guide us, eventually meeting in the bathroom to read.

The rest of the holiday is a succession of memories of dips in a sea that would alternate between being blue, green or transparent. A recollection that does stand out is our encounter with Mimmo, one of the most unique characters that I have ever come across. My father had met Mimmo the day he and my mother had missed the hydrofoil because of the lobster incident. I wasn't there but I can describe what went on with reasonable accuracy. My mother isn't the type to make apologies for herself, especially not when the situation is self-evident, as it was in the case of her predilection for lobster. My father, having realised that it was useless to argue, decided to leave my mother to the pleasures of the table and to devote himself to his favourite hobby, pottering around the marina.

For my father, and in this I take after him, curiosity goes way beyond silent observation and always ends up in minding other people's business. At Cerrinia, for example, when it snowed he would go out on the pretext of a walk, fully equipped with all the gear, and return only after he had helped to fit chains to all the cars he came across, shovelled snow from all the vehicles which had come to a standstill, and viewing all this as pure chance, had invited home those he came across whom he thought most likeable.

He couldn't believe his luck when he heard that a small boat wanted to set sail without a compass and was headed to Vulcano, the same destination he and my mother wished to reach. Rather than wait for the next hydrofoil, my father decided to lend a hand. It must have been a rare foggy day, because a compass wasn't usually needed to navigate from Milazzo to Vulcano, which was easily sighted at only 20 miles from the coast. In any case, my father would have confidently asserted that he would be able to lead them with ease to their destination because he knew that strait by memory. And so my mother – who most certainly could not protest; after all, they had missed the ferry because of her lobster lunch – my father, the 'sea wolf' Mimmo and his blonde girlfriend, reached Vulcano a few hours later. I had gone down to the port with my minder and not finding them there when I arrived waited in tears.

Mimmo was what my mother would call *una macchietta* – a real character. In order to thank my father for the help and hospitality he had received over the course of a few days, he took us to a typical restaurant on Lipari. On the terrace, shaded by a bougainvillea in full flower, there were red onions and cherry tomatoes hung to dry and an intense fragrance of capers. The buds, which had not yet bloomed, would be served in a fresh caper salad, *insalata di capperoni freschi*, seasoned with olive oil, basil, mint and thin slices of lemon. The traditional recipe expects that you will have a caper plant available, whose largest buds will be collected in July and August, but I often make it using salted capers, after they have been left in cold water for two hours then well dried. Capers, like olives, have a bitter taste when they have just been picked and have to be treated before they can be eaten. They should be put in boiling water for a minute then have the water gently squeezed out of them, and left to soak in cold water for two days.

CAPER SALAD

1 cup capers
2 potatoes (boiled with skin on, cut in large pieces)
1 new season onion (or spring onions)
20 small tomatoes (cherry tomatoes)
10 fresh basil leaves
2 sprigs fresh oregano, alternatively 3 mint leaves
8 tablespoons good extra virgin olive oil

capperi

Place washed capers into a salad bowl together with the still warm (that way they'll pick up the aromas), peeled and quartered potatoes, finely sliced onion (previously soaked in vinegar for 10 minutes, then patted dry), halved tomatoes, torn not cut basil leaves (the oxidation process is slower), fresh oregano leaves or small mint leaves – whichever you prefer. Just before serving, dress salad with salt and oil to taste. The version I ate at Lipari had finely sliced lemon in it as well.

scacciapensieri

Lunch would not have been complete without entertainment. Out of nowhere came a man playing a guitar and a *scacciapensieri*[5] and to the rhythm of an almost Arab tune, Mimmo began an unrehearsed striptease on the lunch table, stripping down to his leopard print G-string, much to the somewhat embarrassed delight of my mother.

I have never been back to Vulcano and I am told that it has been ruined by mass tourism, illegal construction and senseless urbanisation. My memory is of an island of extraordinary beauty and intense, surreal colours. Living as we were right on top of a volcano, it felt as if we were close to the earth's core with Vulcano a kind of door between the outside world and the centre of the earth. This is why I feel as if I have heard the earth breathe, something few people can claim to have done.

---

5   Jew's harp – a typical popular folk instrument at the end of the 1900s in Sicily, made out of laminated steel.

CHAPTER SIX

My neighbourhood in Milan

My recollection of the twelve years that we lived in Viale Tunisia is a funny combination of the conflicting emotions which characterise adolescence, ranging from rebellion against one's parents in the search for independence to the experience of stability that comes from belonging to a close-knit family in which everyone feels loved and, most importantly, has the chance to express it.

From home I would take the Number 30 tram which followed the internal ring road and would journey past the city walls of the old part of Milan, built in concentric circles around the original historic centre. When I think of trams now, I still picture them dark green, with wooden sides, winding their way

The old Milano inside the fortified walls.

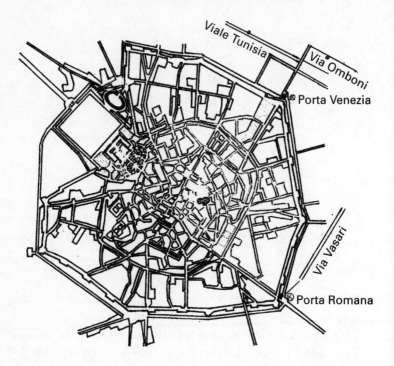

through the tree-lined avenues, almost a guided tour of the city streets. For years now the trams have been orange and long, composed of several loose carriages, and they are as fast as trains, their sides covered with advertising billboards. One last tram of the earlier type remains and it will take you on an interesting sightseeing tour of the historic centre.

Every morning at 7.30, Renato, Monica, Marco and our other friends who were allowed to go to school unaccompanied would be waiting at the tram stop. At that age sneaking a cigarette was the height of adult sophistication. But my father, who never left anything to chance, had managed to create a surveillance system thanks to obliging spies.

In the area of Porta Venezia, which includes Viale Tunisia, all the shops where we did our daily shopping were concentrated around three streets. Initially I would go shopping with my mother or Candida, then subsequently on my own. The arrival of supermarkets had not yet entirely succeeded in displacing the small neighbourhood shops, which in Italy are a fundamental part of our culture. Often when people ask me what I miss about Italy, I reply: 'My fishmonger.' But that is just the tip of the iceberg; if truth be told I especially miss the butcher, the grocer and the baker, not to mention the many other local shopkeepers.

Of all of them, it is Campari the butcher who springs most readily to mind. Funny, considering that I never knew his first name. He was the one who 'tipped' my father off about my bravado in smoking, and I am grateful to him for it now. He came from the countryside near Cremona, a city in the province of Lombardy an hour away from Milan, where pig farming is still an art. He had big thickset hands and wore a typical butcher's cap. His round face was always lit up by a big smile. The white butcher's coat that he always wore with its sleeves rolled up was tight on him, due either to his ample stomach or because he wore several layers underneath to keep him warm. At the sales counter stood his wife, a feminine version of him, and their son, shy, slim, with red hair and lots of freckles. Campari was always busy trimming the meat with precise and careful movements, more akin to those of a goldsmith than a butcher. He would work on a marble bench that he cleaned continually of every trace of blood, letting the enormous knife fall on the thick wooden shelf. Behind him was the door to the cold store, through which you would catch a glimpse of the carcasses.

He fashioned the meat on the bone and the traces of fat in such a way that by the time he had finished every cut had its own unique shape which best suited it for a particular type of cooking. Because of him, for years, right up until I had to learn them at the Cooking Institute, I never knew the names of the different parts of the animal that were best suited to the recipe I had in mind. All

I ever needed to say was: 'Campari, I need to make *vitello tonnato* for four people,' and he would put the finishing touches to the cut of meat, if necessary tying it in a particular way and then passing it over to the loving ministrations of his son who would weigh it on the large red manual scales, in its initial layer of wax paper, and then he would wrap it in another sheet and put it in a plastic bag. There was never a drop of blood in the fridge, never an error in cooking time, calculated on the basis of the recipe and the weight of the meat which Campari took great care in signalling to you as part of the service he provided. He was always extremely careful to throw away only the fat and skin, because every little scrap of meat was given punctually to the soup kitchen that Don Franco ran, the largest and most well equipped in the city. Nearly every evening he would also stay on to prepare and serve dinner to the hundreds of homeless – *barboni* as we called them – who found a little warmth and friendship around Don Franco's table. In her wanderings with the dog in the nearby public gardens of Porta Venezia, my mother had even befriended one of these vagrants whom she preferred to refer to more romantically as a 'bohemian'.

In Italian butcher shops you can also buy *affettati*, cured meat and salami, and these were Campari's real passion. As well as *prosciutto cotto*, and *prosciutto crudo* from Parma or San Daniele, he always had a good stock of different products depending on the season, such as *salame* from Cremona, made by using only the lean and choice cuts of pork, flavoured with garlic and red wine. The *salame* can be up to a metre long and even though it is aged for a long time it always retains a moist consistency and its own characteristic taste. The *luganega* is a prime pork or pork and beef sausage that can be eaten either raw or cooked. There are many different types, all with different names. My mother knows them as *verʒit*, so called because they were eaten with *le verʒe*, Savoy cabbage, during the autumn months. My favourite *salami* as a child were *cacciatorini*. *Cacciatorini* are small, a bit like sausages, and made of a mixture of finely minced beef and pork, with no added seasoning. They have a simple but appetising flavour. Their name comes from the Italian word for hunter, *cacciatore*, because they were the daily diet of the hunters during their long shooting parties.

In the area between Lodi and Cremona, the site of large land-owners' properties in the past, the butcher would go once a year to slaughter the pigs and make sausages with the choicest cuts of meat. The scraps, left-overs and fatty bits would also be made into sausages and given to the peasants who would boil them a few weeks later and eat them with potatoes. This is how *cotechino* came into being, which in Italy is traditionally served with lentils for New Year's Day dinner as a portent of good luck, because lentils represent money according to traditional folklore. The name *cotechino* comes from *coteca* which means skin in Lombard dialect.

SCOTTIGLIA

1 carrot

1 onion

1 celery stick

1 clove garlic

4 tablespoons extra virgin olive oil

700g mixed meats as desired (beef, chicken, veal, pork, rabbit), cut into large cubes or *spezzatino*

1/2 glass red wine

4 fresh ripe tomatoes or 1 can whole peeled tomatoes

100g green beans

1 zucchini

1 capsicum (or better still a quarter cut from each colour of capsicum: red, yellow, orange, green)

salt and pepper

bunch of parsley

bunch of basil

Finely chop the carrot, celery, onion and garlic. Place in a large frying pan – preferably a terracotta one – together with the oil and lightly fry until soft. Add meat and brown. Add the wine and allow to evaporate.

In the meantime, wash remaining vegetables and cut into large pieces about the same size as the meat. Add to frying pan. Cook for approximately 40 minutes, adding a little water if necessary. Add finely chopped parsley and basil just a few minutes before end of cooking.

Serve *scottiglia* on the table accompanied by sliced oven-grilled country-style bread rubbed with garlic and a drizzle of oil.

Originally 'Viale' was the name given to tree-lined city streets, while 'Corso' referred to streets which became filled with flower-adorned carriages or masked youths, or where the Corsa del Palio (horse race) would take place, as in the Via del Corso in Rome – or simply where there was the most pedestrian or road traffic. Nowadays, Viale Tunisia is a main arterial road completely devoid of trees, connecting Piazza della Repubblica with Corso Buenos Aires, with its never-ending stream of cars, bumper to bumper. On the pavements you have to use your elbows to get anywhere, or to see in the windows of the succession of clothes shops, the big department stores like La Rinascente, with its exclusive merchandise, towering up from beneath the arches of the Corso Vittorio Emanuele, next to the Duomo and Pasticceria[1] Motta, famous for its *panettone* and permanently fixed in my mind as the scene of that *merenda* which held so much promise but would never eventuate.

I would have been ten and my cousin Matteo had come to spend the weekend at my place. My *zio* Piero, who was also Matteo's grandfather, had come to visit and promised us *merenda* at Pasticceria Motta which, apart from making *panettone*, was also a fabulous cake shop. And so we set off along Viale Tunisia, where right at the intersection of Corso Buenos Aires you arrived outside

---

1   Confectioners, cake shop.

Pasticceria Motta where you will now find a McDonalds. The display cases of cakes and pastries seemed never-ending, and there we were with our noses glued to the window becoming increasingly indecisive about whether to choose a *bigne' alla crema*, a cream puff with a subtle pale yellow lemon icing; a *pasta frolla mignon*, a miniature wild strawberry tart with its inviting red juice which had also seeped through to the cream under the berries; or the *ventaglietti al miele*. In the latter case, because it was a simple cake made out of puff

pastry and honey, as far as my uncle was concerned, we were allowed to choose two. We accompanied my uncle to the cash register, where having already ordered, he realised that he didn't have his wallet on him! What a disappointment! I can remember the walk home, my cousin and I both utterly dejected and unable to stop feeling sorry for ourselves. We no longer had time to go back to Pasticceria Motta.

In front of Pasticceria Motta where now there is a bank, in those days there was a big furrier on three floors named Pellicceria Collini. I had accompanied my mother, who was carrying a big package wrapped in thick and shiny dark green paper that contained the present my father had given her the day before. I can remember seeing her reflection in the large mirror opposite my bedroom as she stood enveloped in a floor-length white fur coat. Her tanned face, her hands and her feet were the only parts of her that were visible. My mother seemed lost for words, though every now and then she would murmur under her breath, 'Nini, tu sei matto!' – 'Nini, you are crazy!' as she admired that elegant reversible coat made of ermine and mink. My father loved to give extravagant and above all unexpected presents; he never remembered birthdays or anniversaries. Much as my mother loved surprises, she could not bring herself to accept presents that were too expensive. And so it came to pass that after spending a few hours in front of the mirror stroking the beautiful white fur, she had decided to take it back to the shop. I had never been into a furrier before and that day left a big impression on me, the magnificence of the carpets, the antique mirrors, the ornate light fittings, the obsequious attentions of the shop assistants, but above all the unfamiliar smell of the fur and leather. Nowadays when furriers are becoming increasingly scarce (thank goodness), that same smell can be found in shoe shops and in the small hide and leather workshops like the *bottega artigiana* (artisan's workshop) which I am so fond of, situated only a few feet way from the old Pellicceria Collini.

My mother remembers when she was a child, munching on chocolate biscuits on the balcony of the first floor of her Aunt Angelina's house while watching the decorated Carnevale[2] floats go by. Angelina was the peculiar aunt, the one we always referred to in order to illustrate the eccentricities of our family because of her habit of wandering about with a goose on a leash.

Carnevale is celebrated throughout Italy and lasts nearly a week, which varies from year to year but which coincides with the last week before Lent, a time of Easter preparations and of prayer and abstinence from revelry. They are all feast days culminating in Sabato Grasso, the Saturday before Lent, with the parade of floats and of the Maschere – masked characters, representative of

---

2   Carnevale is an early popular festival still celebrated in many parts of Europe today. It is based on a comic inversion of the social order, where the poor imitate the rich. Apart from being a time of festivity, Carnevale functioned as a sociopolitical safety valve allowing the masses to express themselves and poke fun at the rich in a non-threatening context.

each city. These characters are an inheritance of
the Commedia Dell'Arte[3], and were later adopted
by dramatists such as Carlo Goldoni in Italy and
Molière in France.

Venice is characterised by Arlecchino, with
his costume of multicoloured cloth; he is a
cunning and acrobatic manservant, a liar
and a womaniser. Naples has Pulcinella,
dressed from head to toe in white and with
a mask with a large hooked nose, the
embodiment of the typical Neapolitan,

Pulcinella

who approaches life philosophically and who
expresses his emotions in song. Milan is
represented by Meneghino, a typical
servant to the 18th century Spanish aris-
tocracy. He is a man of the people and is
devoted to his masters but is also a bit
self-interested, more out of a need to
feed his family than due to a bad
character. He is proud to be a
native of Milan, so much so that
over the centuries *Meneghino*
has become synonymous with
'Milanese'. He wears the clothes of the man in the street, a brown
jacket edged with red, a gaudily coloured shirt, breeches and striped
socks and a wig with a ponytail. He doesn't wear a mask, but instead
has white and red designs painted on his face.

Meneghino

---

3 The Commedia Dell'Arte originated in Italy in the middle of the 1500s and
   marks the beginning of modern theatre in Europe, with the first professional
   actors.

Nonna Elsa and Nonno Innocente's wedding, 1927.

My mother's family home is found on one of the streets that intersects with Corso Buenos Aires. Her family, the Aliprandis, can be traced back to the 1200s. My grandfather, Innocente, a doctor from an old and noble Milanese family, had married my grandmother Elsa, who was much younger than him. After an adventurous honeymoon, some of which was undertaken in a biplane, an unusual and risky enterprise in those days, they never left Milan again except for the period during the war when they had to be evacuated to Maggio in Valsassina in the mountains above Lecco. After the Second World War and the consequent loss of the majority of the family property, my grandfather had the family home built in the 1950s and it still stands today, full of memories and with its own particular charm.

The austere front door is made of wood and framed by two

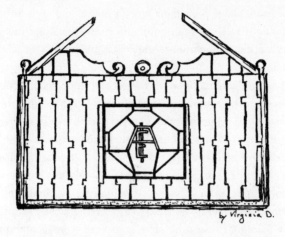

by Virginia D.

marble columns resting on two spheres of black marble. The front entranceway is divided into two by a beautiful wrought-iron gate with my grandparent's initials in gilded brass. A heavy portal occupies the whole rear wall and is made of iron and thick glass that provides access to the internal courtyard that is paved but has no garden. From the concierge's lodge that is small and dark, three small steps covered in a dark red heavy velvet fabric secured by means of a row of shiny brass sections lead to the mezzanine floor where you will find the lift and the stairs. The walls are inlaid with Venetian geometric designs in red; these have only just recently been restored and continue right up to the *piano nobile*. This was the name given to the first floor, the most lavishly decorated, as could be seen from the generous balcony on the front of the building, the only one with floral plaster motifs. It's funny how the perception of value changes over time; in the real estate market these days it is the upper floors that are most sought after. The lift is faithful to the period, enclosed in a wrought-iron steel cage, with elegant small decorative feet made of brass, set into the worn marble of the floor. The feature I like the most is the letterbox, even though nowadays it is ill-suited to the volume and size of the mail that arrives on a daily basis. But those small brass plates with their wavy borders and stylised writing reminded me of my grandmother's recipe book and my grandfather's critical annotations, which I still come across now in his old books.

My grandparents lived on the second floor, where you came across the two entrances, separated by a low wrought-iron gate, one leading to my grandfather's surgery and the other to the house. The surgery, which is still used as such today, has a waiting room, a small dark hall that leads to a room my grandfather used as a laboratory for running tests, a small windowless bathroom and his consulting room. This was dominated by a complete human skeleton, subsequently donated to a deserving faculty of medicine, and a painting illustrating an unconscious woman supported by two figures, one shrouded in black and a man in a white shirt, symbolising the medical profession's continual struggle to snatch life from death's embrace, a sombre present from my *zia* Lilia. I still haven't found the right spot for this painting in my house and none of us have continued in the medical profession, a family tradition for generations that so far has stopped at *nonno* Innocente. There were lots of medical books in the glass-fronted cupboards and my grandfather would sometimes slip banknotes into them which he received from his patients and which over time his daughters would learn to find, profiting from the absentmindedness of their father. There was also a writing desk, now in *zia* Lilia's house, the only one of the sisters who had always lived there, and on it were two objects that now sit on the card table in my mother's living room. These are two small glasses made of thick glass with small engraved bronze lids that once held ink and water for dipping the fountain pen.

The apartment consisted of various rooms along a windowless corridor consistent with the typical layout of the period. The 'empire' sitting room took its name from its period furniture; the green room was so named because of its pale greenish tapestry; and then there was the dining room. There were three bedrooms.

In the one used for games, with a doll's house that even though I have never seen it remains as one of my permanent childhood fantasies, was the wardrobe which holds so much linen that it still meets the needs of the whole extended family. There were also two bathrooms and a kitchen.

The rooms that face the street get the most light and are also better cared for as they are the ones used for entertaining. The windows that go all the way up to the extremely high ceiling have wide wooden frames. The doors are inlaid with wood and the walls are covered with *boiserie*. In the main living room there is a French door that opens out onto a tiny marble terrace, and on the window-sill there is a fixed iron rod on which the flag of the newly created Italian Republic would be hoisted. On the other side of the corridor the rooms don't get as much light because they face onto the internal courtyard. The kitchen wasn't particularly big, partly because there weren't a lot of kitchen appliances and cooking was seen as a necessity rather than a pleasure. However, in the kitchen there was a big cage full of doves, raised for pure pleasure and not for culinary purposes. The only other animals in the Aliprandi household were Gianmutanda – 'John in underpants'. The girls had chosen this name because even though the dog was a bitch, when she was in heat my grandmother would put underpants on her. There was also a hen. When it got old, my grandmother decided to use her to make stock, complying with popular wisdom which says that *gallina vecchia fa buon brodo* – old hens make good broth. My grandmother could not find anyone willing to kill the hen, not even my grandfather, the doctor in residence, who naturally had some experience of death. So *nonna* Elsa, who must have been a determined woman, took action herself. After she had given its neck a good wringing, having followed the instructions she received from a farmworker, she left it in the courtyard ready for plucking the following day, when it was found still alive and scratching around with its long neck.

Thanks to his profession as a doctor, my grandfather enjoyed the privilege of the continual availability of food of every type and which, at a time before refrigerators, was kept fresh by means of ice regularly delivered by *quel del giazz*,[4] as the ice seller was called in dialect. Apart from the fresh eggs that arrived on a daily basis, there were rabbits and chickens and every so often there would be a hare. Preparing hare was an opportunity for celebration. Once it had been skinned and cleaned of its internal organs it was hung at the door of the little room off the courtyard. This was done to let the meat ripen and so tenderise it. It would then be marinated for three days in red wine and vegetables and cooked like this in an oval copper pot at least 1 metre in diameter, over a special fire lit in the courtyard. Less appealing is an account of how black pudding is prepared; it is made from the blood taken from a chicken and cooked with a large quantity of onion. According to my mother, its taste is similar to *fegato alla veneta*, a typical Venetian dish of liver cooked with plenty of onions. The thought of such a

quel del giazz

copper-pot repairer

dish these days may seem disgusting, not to mention the obscene method of extracting the blood from a tiny incision made behind the chicken's ear. But during the war, hunger was the main enemy that the civilian populace found themselves fighting. This was an extremely real childhood memory for my mother and, if for no other reason than that, is worthy of respect.

The *cazzoeula*, the name probably originating from *cazoo*, the dialect word for ladle, is a typical recipe eaten by Milanese families and appears with variations in other Italian regions. It is a rich

---

4   *Quello del ghiaccio* in Italian, meaning the one who sells ice.

dish, typically eaten in winter and using all the produce available in this part of Italy during that season: Savoy cabbage, which is frost-resistant, and pork left-overs after the pig has been butchered. The best parts of this precious animal (*del maiale non si butta via niente* – every part of a pig is useful – is a saying you still hear today) were used to make *salami* and sausages and what remained were the scraps, the hide, the knees, the ribs, the head and the feet. The ideal accompaniment for *cazzoeula* was *polenta*, which my mother still makes in the same way in one of the many pots from that kitchen.

I never knew my grandparents, but from my mother's stories, from the photos and from the notorious characteristics of the family members, I have constructed a picture of them that is dear to me. My grandfather Innocente, a stern man and a disciplinarian, must most certainly have had a few headaches bringing up three girls in the postwar years of great change. Mirella, my mother, and Mary,

Zia Mary and Mum at Madesino, 1963. Mum was pregnant with me.

Above: Mum and Dad at a ball on one of their first formal dates.

Left: Mum and Dad's wedding day, 1962.

the youngest, are physically very similar. With long jet-black hair and extremely dark brown eyes they are tall and slim and their long legs have such slender ankles that my grandfather called them *garetti* – horses' ankles. They are the exact opposite of the Emilian legs I have inherited from my father's family. Lilia, the eldest, is very different both physically and temperamentally. They all have the large nose that I have had passed down to me, along with the saying *brutto naso non guasta bel viso* – an ugly nose doesn't ruin a pretty face – and a loud speaking voice which they justify as being a result of the fact that as *nonno* Innocente got older he became increasingly hard of hearing.

My grandmother would say that my mother was a real tomboy, a well-deserved reputation according to the stories my mother told us. Attempting to escape one of my grandfather's rages she climbed up the lamppost risking electrocution. As a punishment, she was locked in her room, where she had the bright idea of escaping by jumping out of the window using only an open umbrella as her parachute. Luckily her room was only on the first floor and the heavy snowfall cushioned her impact. Nevertheless my grandmother decided to get to the heart of the matter and devout Catholic that she was, determined to take my mother along to the local church for a blessing and a good telling-off. One of my mother's nicknames was *la commediante pentita* – the repentant comedienne – because of her ability to make herself cry at will or simulate fainting fits at the most opportune moments. It must be in the genes, because my daughter Martha is already showing the first signs of having inherited this gift from her grandmother. At least *nonna* Elsa managed to channel my mother's energy into sport, and so it was that at fifteen she met my father, who was seventeen at the time, at the tennis club. The photos of that period show him to be slim with fair hair and green eyes and a clever and lively expression, which in adulthood would transform into a penetrating gaze that gave the impression that absolutely nothing escaped him. His secretaries referred to him as

Mum at 15 years old.

'the architect with the icy stare'. But if his gaze seemed cold, his voice was deep and warm and often became a resounding laugh that was irresistible. In the evening when I was in bed just before falling asleep I would hear that laugh emerging from the living room which was always full of their friends and it made me feel all warm inside, something I still experience to this day when I close my eyes and conjure up that familiar laugh. He had a strong and resolute character and, unlike my mother, had grown up free of the influence of an authoritarian father. He used to tell us about the first time he was invited to my mother's house, for my mother's fifteenth birthday party, and my grandfather was there standing guard at the living room door, making sure that everyone was behaving themselves. Later, with the excuse of popping out to get some cigarettes, my father disappeared from that house without a trace for ten years.

Nor did my father become any more compliant with age; my mother always had a hard time getting him to accept *nonno* Innocente's rules. But my father knew how to handle himself, like the time when in order to avoid the complications of their official engagement dinner, he presented my mother with her engagement ring at the front door! Among the many wedding preparations which my father was unable to avoid altogether was my mother's attendance at Don Micio's Scuola per Fidanzate, or Fiancée School. My mother can only remember two of the lessons: one on the importance of taking care of one's feet, because her future husband might at any moment experience an uncontrollable urge to kiss them, and one where she learnt how to make Sicilian cassata, which she still makes every Christmas.

FIANCÉE SCHOOL CASSATA

Traditionally a Sicilian recipe, with Arab origins, *cassata* is made up of layers of sponge dipped in milk and liqueur, and layers of ricotta mixed with candied fruit and chunks of chocolate.

300g dry sponge cake (without crust and at least 2 days old)
thick waxed paper (found in specialised kitchen stores)
350ml milk
3 tablespoons rum
2 tablespoons rose water
3 tablespoons Maraschino liqueur (or cherry liqueur)
300g *ricotta*
100g white sugar
100g dark chocolate cut into small cubes (do not use small chips)
100g mixed candied fruits (citrus peel and red cherries)
fruit cake container (approx. 20cm x 12cm or large enough to
    accommodate 3 layers of sponge and 2 layers of ricotta mixture)

Cut the sponge cake lengthwise in slices of about 1cm thick. Divide these slices into 3 groups. Line cake container with the waxed paper, allowing a little extra to overlap the sides.

Pour half the milk, 3 tablespoons of rum and 1 tablespoon of rose water into a bowl. Set aside. Pour remaining milk together with the cherry liqueur and the rose water into another bowl. Set aside.

Mix *ricotta* together with the sugar until creamy, then put in a bowl and add the cubed chocolate and candied fruits.

Using one group of sponge slices, dunk (taking care not to overdo as they will be too soggy) into the rum/milk mixture and line the bottom of the container. Lightly press down with your hands. Cover with *ricotta* mixture then a layer of sponge slices dunked in the milk/cherry liqueur mixture. Repeat with another layer of the ricotta mixture and a final layer of sponge slices dipped in rum/milk. Freeze well before serving.

One of the aromas which stirs my memories of Christmas and its anticipation, the latter most acutely felt when you are a child, is the fragrance of freshly baked *panettone* that blows gently across the whole city on days where there is a light wind, from November on, and originating from the factory in the city centre. The *panettone* comes in a light blue box decorated with a picture of the Duomo of Milan. Inside, wrapped in dark cellophane you will find the authentic *panettone* of Milan, never iced, full of raisins and fragrant with eggs, butter and candied orange and lemon peel.

Nowadays, after many attempts, corrections and failures, I manage to reproduce at home a *panettone* that, while perhaps not having quite the same shape or consistency, does have the same fragrant smell of the *panettone* of my olfactory memory.

A week before Christmas the *biga* is prepared. This is a mixture of water and flour and must be kneaded at length then wrapped tightly in a piece of white cloth and left to rise for 24 hours. Then you add flour and water and work the dough again, kneading the dough at length and beating it against the table to facilitate the formation of the gluten. You repeat the process again over the course of a few days. The whole family participates in this process; it is a sort of pre-Christmas ritual. My daughters Martha and Giulia are able to knead the dough and they gain great pleasure from taking it in turns to beat it with a rolling pin. Paolo's part in all this is at the delicate phase when all the other ingredients are added – eggs, butter, sugar and mixed candied fruit – when the dough reaches a size and consistency which makes it difficult for just one person to work.

Once the mixture has been left to rise in paper casings the wait begins. You pass to the baking stage when the fragrance of the *panettone* attracts even the most reserved neighbours to the house. A slice of *panettone* with a cup of real Italian coffee is by now their accepted right.

Christmas with my parents involved the whole family respecting the old saying, *'Natale con i tuoi, Pasqua con chi vuoi'* – 'Spend Christmas with your relatives and Easter with whoever you want', and always managed to be a time which found us together around the Christmas tree. When *nonna* Tina was still alive, she would without any help cook *tortellini* and *cotechino* for all present. She would prepare twenty *tortellini* per person and ninety for my father who was extremely partial to them. As a rule they should be cooked in chicken broth. Entering her house in the days before Christmas was a real experience, at the front door you would smell the *pasta all'uovo* that had been left to dry and covered all the benches in the entire house, including the storeroom. My mother took care of decorating the tree and this would take a few days, but the result was really something special. She would hang the Christmas decorations that she had inherited from her mother with such love. I remember in particular a large pink ball decorated with golden threads and a smaller gold one. It is my sister Giudi who has inherited my mother's artistic flair and who maintains the tradition of decorating the Christmas tree. In recent years she has introduced her own particular decorative style and nowadays it is often not a fir tree that serves as a structure for the decorations but sometimes a branch of dried wood and other times transparent threads hung across the ceiling. The decorations themselves are imaginative and truly amazing and she conjures them up out of nothing.

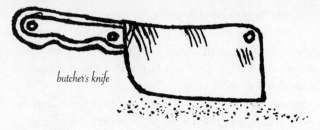

butcher's knife

On Christmas Eve the *panettone* would be eaten on its own, dipped in *spumante*, while for Christmas lunch it would be filled with a creamy *ricotta* mix containing pieces of dark chocolate. My mother would remove the top of the *panettone* and scoop out the interior, then she would make a filling by mixing together *ricotta*, egg yolks, sugar, rum and dark chocolate pieces – bitter, very Italian, not Swiss or Belgian. Real Italian chocolate is made without milk or other ingredients and must contain more than 60 per cent cocoa. With a butcher's knife – which is the generic name for all the professional knives used in Italian kitchens – my mother would gouge out pieces of chocolate from the large 1kg tablets of chocolate that you buy at the supermarket. A Milanese tradition requires you to keep the *panettone* until San Biagio's day, the patron saint of the throat, in order to protect oneself against the ills of the coldest months.

GLOSSARY:

PANETTONE (pah-neht-to-ne) is a Christmas cake originating in Milan but which has now been adopted all over Italy. As legend would have it, it was created towardss the end of the 15th century at the court of a Milanese nobleman, Ludovico Il Moro (the Moor). The recipe evolved into its final form in the middle of the 19th century. It consists of flour, butter, eggs, sugar and raisins, slowly fermented and shaped into a large *pane* or loaf; the suffix *-one* in Italy means large, hence *panettone* or large loaf.

PROSCIUTTO SAN DANIELE is produced in the same way as *prosciutto crudo di parma* but it comes from San Daniele in Friuli region.

RICOTTA (ree-cot-tah) is not a proper cheese, but it is made from the whey left over from the production of cheese. The name means twice-cooked because the whey is heated a second time. *Ricotta* is not salted and has virtually no calories. Its texture and taste varies depending on the type of milk used (goat, cow or sheep). Italians use *ricotta* for filling a short pastry base making a low-fat and delicious 'cheese-cake'.

CHAPTER SEVEN

The fragrance of basil

Basil will always be associated with my summer holidays at Santa Margherita Ligure or, as the regulars call it, 'Santa', where *zia* Luciana had a holiday home that she sold only a few years ago. The house is right in the centre of the town on the road that leads to Nozarego, a small village off the tourist track where one can enjoy a stunning view of the Gulf of Tigullio. In this village there was a simple bar that served a delicious apple cake, perfect for those holiday breakfasts. One of the things I love about my husband Paolo is that he has a mother like Virginia, who among numerous other things has given me an apple cake recipe that takes me back to the ivy-covered terrace where I would eat breakfast in summer.

basilico

VIRGINIA'S APPLE CAKE

100g plain flour
100g self-raising flour
100g sugar
3 whole eggs
milk
1kg apples

Place first 4 ingredients in a bowl and add enough milk to obtain a liquid batter – similar to yoghurt or mayonnaise in consistency.

Peel and slice apples. Layer slices evenly on the base of an oven dish. Pour over the egg mixture.

Decorate top with more sliced apples in an overlapping fan pattern.

Bake in a preheated oven at 120°C until golden brown.

Normally I double the recipe for a rectangular 23–25cm x 33–35cm cake tin.

The asphalt road goes as far as Nozarego, but from here on the paths crisscross though the internal hills of Olmi, from Portofino Vetta to San Fruttuoso, points of interest on the track through the Monte di Portofino nature reserve. The fragrance of the wild oregano found there mixes with that of the borage used as a filling for the local ravioli, *panzotti*, and with the scent of the grapes, the figs, and in particular the basil, which is ever-present in Liguria, even though it doesn't grow wild.

i fichi

Basil grows in the vegetable gardens found everywhere in these uncharted hills. Hidden by a dense vegetation and known to only a handful of people, the houses of old peasant families can be found side by

LIGURIA REGION

Genova

Santa Margherita L.

Rapallo

Paraggi

San Fruttuoso

Portofino

Sestri Levante

Riva Trigoso

Golfo del Tigullio

Le Cinque Terre

side with the villas of the wealthy inhabitants of Genoa. The track leads into the forest, but the forest is neither dense nor dark. The light is so intense that it bleaches the colours and endows the landscape with a surreal quality. It wouldn't surprise me at all if a gnome popped out from behind a tree. I could wander these paths with my eyes closed, allowing myself to be led by my sense of smell and nothing else.

Near the tiny chapel, Cappella delle Gave, the sea bursts through the pines and on summer days the sun turns it a cobalt blue. The road that goes from Santa Margherita to Portofino lies just below, but it is hidden from view and the noise of the cars that pass without stopping doesn't reach the water's edge. The sea seems so close you could dive right in, and then why not climb back up to the beach huts of the Covo di

Nord Est, one of the most fashionable and well-known bars of the seventies and eighties, the perfect meeting place for the evening apéritif.

The path continues until it forks, one branch leading up towards the mountain, the other going down to the Bay of Paraggi. The bay is a small and narrow cove, right beneath the road that after just a few more bends arrives at Portofino. A couple of hundred metres away you come across two hotels, a handful of restaurants that attract the tourist trade and three *stabilimenti balneari*.[1] Two are constructed almost entirely on foundations and terraces made of wood. The Carillon is one of these. For years, every summer in July and August we rented a beach cabin and a sun umbrella, the last in the row, sheer above the sea, and every year we would reacquaint ourselves with the same families from Milan and Genoa, and Sergio the gallant lifeguard.

The lifeguard plays a special role in Italian society. Most of our beaches are equipped with privately owned *stabilimenti balneari* and run by one or more lifeguards who open the sun umbrellas when it's sunny and close them at sunset. They hire out the pedal boats, keep an eye on the children splashing about in the water and on the boys playing footy on the beach and annoying the women sunbathing. For the many who return every year to the same resort, the lifeguard becomes a trusted presence, but popular imagination has also painted him in the more lascivious role of a ladies' man who preys on women alone on vacation. It's hard to believe when you actually see the lifeguards, who rarely look anything like those in *Baywatch*.

Every time I get to Santa Margherita I stop by to see Sergio, who never changes – tanned all year round, with blue eyes and

1 Going to the beach in Italy is a fairly formal and well-organised experience. There is *spiaggia libera*, the 'free beach' open to all, but most Italians will pay for the facilities that a *stabilimento balneare* – a bathing establishment – has to offer: beach chairs, changing rooms, lifeguards and a regularly cleaned stretch of beach.

curly, ruffled, grey hair, always barefoot, wearing short shorts and an elegant T-shirt. He used to enjoy hanging out with us teenagers; with his own particular brand of *savoir faire*, pausing to exhale smoke from his ever-present cigarette, he would tell us about his latest female conquests. But let's face it, most men, especially Italian men, think they are ladykillers.

When my father, who would only entertain the idea of the sea if on a boat, found himself landlocked, he preferred to remain in the company of the many Genovesi[2] present at the little tables in the open air on the terrace above the sea. I would hear his booming laugh even when I was in the water. Free of the commitments and formality of city life, he would give free rein to his personality, which was a combination of a carefree cheerfulness, characteristic of the natives of Emilia, and the biting sarcasm typical of the inhabitants of Arezzo. I like to remember him in his bathing suit, the only one on the beach without a tan, while he drank the espresso that Sergio made so well.

My mother loved it, because every year she would be reunited with the same friends and because it was possible, despite being dressed only in your swimsuit, to take shelter during the hottest part of the day inside the bar which in the evenings became a nightclub, but during the day served simple but good food. A nice plate of *prosciutto e melone* was always available.

This is a typical Italian summer dish, now found in every part of the country. The orange 'half moons' of melon, juicy and sweet, wrapped in the salty red slices of *prosciutto*, are to be found in every outdoor buffet by the sea, party by the pool or lakeside, or breakfast eaten in city courtyards. *Prosciutto* and melon embody many aspects of Italian culture: the coupling of the juicy sweet melon with the fragrant *prosciutto*, lightly salted and of indisputable quality; the juxtaposition of the two colours reminiscent of

---

2   Inhabitants of Genoa.

the sun and an example of the best that Italian style has to offer; the yellow-orange of the slices of Pachino[3] melon, with their soft but compact consistency making them the perfect accompaniment for the intense Indian red of the *prosciutto di Parma* that is thinly sliced and silky to the touch. Melons are a summer fruit and *prosciutto di Parma* is found all over Italy. You don't need to be an expert to verify its quality. The *salumiere* will be quite happy for you to try a piece. If it has a nice deep red colour and a sweet taste, it is definitely of good quality. Experts are able to identify the *prosciutto*'s origin and maturity; some maintain they can even tell which of the pig's haunches has been used. It would appear that the pig has a tendency to carry its weight on the right trotter, which makes that leg fattier and less flavoursome!

This dish requires next to no preparation: all you have to do is clean the melon by removing its seeds, slice it and unwrap the *prosciutto*. However, the unwrapping of the *prosciutto* can take some time if it has been bought at one of the more elegant *salumeria*. In the latter case, the slices of *prosciutto* will have been artistically placed on a white paper tray (gold paper trays are used for *pasticcini*), each layer separated by a sheet of greaseproof paper. The whole thing is then wrapped in paper bearing the name of the prize-winning *salumeria* and duly tied with a ribbon. The paper used is actually a strong aluminium foil, while the *pasticcerie* use either white or pink paper.

While preparing the dish, one or two slices will always break. The rules of *buon gusto*[4] dictate that you do not use them, but eat them instead.

The Bay of Paraggi is dominated by the castle Bonomi Bassetti that extends out over the rocks and seems to merge with them. The

---

3 Pachino is a village in Sicily where the most sought-after melons are grown.

4 Literally 'good taste', but used here with a double meaning. The broken slices taste good, but it is also 'in good taste' not to put them on the dish being served.

stretch of sea that surrounds the bay was closed to motorboats, which can't go beyond the chain attached to the two cliffs that mark the confines of the bay. The castle sits on the cliff to the east and it would be about 100 metres from the shore to the chain. Every morning I would swim out to the chain and perch on it for long periods to watch the boats moored nearby. Then I would return to the shore, stopping for a moment right beneath the castle. At that spot there was a cluster of rocks that could be climbed with some difficulty, but where you could dive into the deep emerald-coloured waters. For many years I renounced the comfort of the bathing resort, preferring these crowded rocks, close enough to keep my mother happy, but far enough away from her constant scrutiny. Around eleven in the morning the gang would meet. How I envied those who appeared still half asleep, the result of having spent a 'fantastic' night out doing mundane things, unexciting to all except those of us who didn't have the same freedom. Their stories, full of unlikely but fascinating adventures, occupied the breaks between dips in the sea that provided respite from the heat of the sun and the tanning process. Sometimes the result was a condition that my mother would call 'potato' sunburn, not because I looked like the vegetable in question but because the burnt part would be covered with slices of raw potato which considerably alleviated the pain and stopped it getting any worse.

When I was sixteen I was finally allowed to go out at night but had to be back by 11 p.m. on the dot. There was no way I could be late because my mother would wait up for me.

The gang would meet at Gelateria Frigerio in Rapallo. In those days I wasn't worried about watching my weight. One of the specialities that the *gelaterie* launched at the time was ice-cream spaghetti, tomato or pesto flavoured, and 'fried eggs'.

ICE-CREAM 'SPAGHETTI'

vanilla ice-cream
200g plain sponge cake
mint or berry syrup

Allow the ice-cream to soften slightly, then put through a potato ricer to make 'spaghetti'. The base for the sauce is made with crumbled sponge cake flavoured with either a red berry or mint syrup.

I have also developed an alcoholic version by using cherry liqueur.

'FRIED EGGS' GELATO

1 packet vanilla ice-cream
1 tin halved peaches in syrup
crème patissière

Allow ice-cream to soften slightly, then using a spatula spread the ice-cream into low mounds on individual plates. Place two peach halves (cavity side down) on each ice-cream serving – hence the 'eggs'. Pour a thin line of *crème patissière* (custard) around the edges to imitate melted butter.

Giorgio, Mariano and I were a regular threesome. Giorgio had a legendary Lancia Fulvia, just big enough for three people. He was always experimenting with his driving skills when it came time to take me home. To this end, every evening we would leave just a little bit later, with the foreseeable outcome that I wouldn't be allowed to go out the next evening. The whole gang, often more than twenty of us, would go in search of small restaurants inland and around Rapallo, where it was possible to sit outside in the fresh air, often in the middle of olive groves, and with the excuse of having something to drink, try the specialities of the area. One of my favourite places was the Arenella which at the time was a bar, restaurant and also a beach resort, but which is just a restaurant now, and was located right on the beach of Zoagli, 5km away from Rapallo. We came across it by accident. Zoagli is a tiny and very old *borgo* or hamlet, famous for its silk-velvet weaving workshops. Hidden among the vegetation you would glimpse the numerous Saracen lookout towers, some of which have now been transformed into sumptuous villas. Access to Zoagli is by means of a narrow road off the Via Aurelia,[5] with a sudden bend that winds its way down an extremely steep descent and brings you to the main car park, only a stone's throw from the beach: a narrow strip of sand with two bathing resorts and a 'free' beach the size of a postage stamp, under the high bridge which is sometimes used by the railways. Rising up behind us was the bizarre 17th century 'castle' which the writer Sem Benelli had built.

Zoagli is famous for its *passeggiata dell'amore* or Lovers' Promenade, a walkway that runs along the rocks at sea level, becoming inaccessible as soon as the sea gets rough. Turning your back to the sea, the *passeggiata dell'amore* (the same name as the more famous promenade of the Cinque Terre) is found on your right, but on moonless evenings it is difficult to locate

---

5   The Via Aurelia, along with the Via Emilia and Via Cassia, are the main arterial roads in Italy that date back to Roman times.

the short flight of steps which give access to it.

We went off in the opposite direction, not having found the entranceway, and carrying on walking beyond a tiny beach bordered by rocks found ourselves under the wooden terraces of the Arenella beach resort, whose lights illuminated a stretch of transparent sea. This was where the rowboats were drawn up out of the sea in the evenings. The small waves washed the pebbles against the shoreline, creating a pleasant sound, amplified by the creaking of the wooden beams above us. The ideal moment for an evening swim! While someone took our order, Mariano, Giorgio and I dived into the sea. The lights from the bar were not strong enough to illuminate the water's depths where the rocks were and where you could find sea urchins or alternatively end up with their spines in your foot. Luckily for the rest, only one of us paid the price. While we enjoyed the fresh sea urchins with lemon and with their dangerous shells removed, Mariano was absorbed in the impossible task of removing an endless number of painful spines from the soles of his feet. I can't remember how long it took to get the victim back on his feet, but I do recall the golden colour and wonderful aroma of the fried fish or *fritto misto*, a dish found in all seaside restaurants. The fish are smaller than an anchovy, but larger than whitebait. They are eaten whole and there is no need to remove their heads, tails or bones. The dish was served on a huge platter in the middle of the table, with everyone helping themselves. And there would always be a bottle of Pigato, a good local white wine, chilled and smelling of the sea.

The drive home that night was quite special. The car exited the tunnel at the entrance of an old villa that has always fascinated me. The surrounding wall is made out of huge blocks of stone which give it the look of a Scottish castle, while the ivy which completely covers the façade makes it seem more like a country house. Around the bend the moon reappeared, its light fading because it was already high in the sky. I could feel the salt on my skin and our laughter echoing in my ears, and can still taste the fried fish and

basilico

smell the fragrant chilled light wine. I wasn't sure exactly what time it was, since I never wore a watch, but I knew my mother would be waiting up for me. But tonight, the sea urchins had given me a good excuse for making her laugh and this time I was off the hook.

In this part of Liguria, basil is often found in the snacks that accompany the apéritif. It's present in the pizzas, made with slices of toasted bread and pieces of heavy red *costoluto* tomato, in the flat white *focaccetta*, dripping with a light oil, and in the marinated anchovies. In the years before *zia* Luciana had bought her house, we rented an apartment in an old villa in traditional Genovese architectural style, whose garden backed onto the Villa Durazzo, one of the splendid residences belonging to the Genovese nobility. Originally built on a hill as a 'house with a turret', in the early 6th century it became transformed into an aristocratic residence. Its terrace with its fantastic panorama is decorated with rows of statues along the balustrade and the driveway is bordered with multicoloured hydrangeas. In the grounds of the Villa, the property of the council of Santa Margherita since 1973 and now a public park, classical music concerts are held throughout the summer. We would enjoy the sun, the cool of the evening and the concert, sitting comfortably in our garden, sipping cold peach tea, made by my mother with the addition of a few mint leaves and a piece of cucumber with the skin removed.

In those two years my mother dedicated herself with fierce ardour to various culinary experiments. For example, she would insist on buying fresh anchovies instead of ones that had already been preserved. She would slit them open and as tiny as they were, she would remove their heads and clean them of their bones and entrails and then she would put them in jars and cover them with layers of salt. Then after two nerve-wracking days she would throw them in the rubbish bin, because instead of marinating they had gone off. The smell, however, lingered in the house for some time. It was much easier to buy them at the fish market. The fish market at Santa Margherita is located under the porticos on the sea front. When the sun sets it is pleasant to wait for the return of the fishing boats, which sell their catch, varying from season to season, even in the early morning.

The scent of basil is found even here, this time issuing from the Caffé del Porto, a proper restaurant now, but which only two years ago served just apéritifs with an endless range of local specialities such as *focaccia* with cheese, onions, or olives, thin slices of raw swordfish marinated in lemon, which intensifies its pinkish flesh, *ʒucchini* and stuffed peppers and *pesto alla Genovese*.

It is important to clarify here that we are talking about *pesto Genovese* style. First of all, the basil itself: the leaves should be very small and the aroma intense and sweet, not pungent and slightly minty like the variety I most often find in Milan. According to my friend Orazio, whose family have been grocers for generations at

mortar & pestle

Pegli, the best basil comes from the Valley of Sestri Ponente, west of Genoa, and only grows in an area of a few square kilometres. The leaves need to be picked in the early morning, when they are still moist and firm from the night's dew. The basil shouldn't be washed, as the leaves are extremely delicate. If necessary clean them with a damp cloth. A gentle pat will do, just enough to remove any residual earth. The expert doesn't need to be told this, since it holds true for mushrooms as well as basil. Gently grind the leaves in a mortar and pestle, gradually adding the fresh garlic clove, the pine nuts and a good quality olive oil. It goes without saying that these last two ingredients should 'speak the same language' as the basil. At this point we are faced with the age-old dilemma of which cheese to use. In Santa Margherita they say a little *prescinsoa* or quark should be used, but only a few kilometres away it's not used at all. However, everyone does agree that *pecorino* should be used in the same quantity as, or instead of, Parmigiano Reggiano, which is obviously foreign as it comes from another region altogether.

✦

PESTO SANS FRONTIÈRES

2 basil plants (100g leaves)
40g pine nuts (any nuts will do, but never use peanuts!)
1 clove fresh garlic (remove the internal stalk which tends to make the
    pesto indigestible)
1 cup (200ml) top quality extra virgin olive oil
a few crystals rock salt
1 tablespoon quark
pecorino or Grano Padano to taste

Not only is basil a summer plant, but its vibrant green colour reminds me of sunlight, which is why I try and preserve the green of the leaves as much as possible. I find the colour of the basil therapeutic and inviting for those who consume it.

The trick is to handle the leaves with great care. Wash them if you must, but do it quickly and dry them in a salad spinner. Use a blender with a small bowl and put it in the freezer for ten minutes or so first. This, along with adding rock salt and oil, slows down the oxidation process. Blend the garlic and pine nuts, then transfer them to a jar or whatever you will be using to store the *pesto*. Next blend the basil, but not all of it at once, just as much as the blender can take, together with a few grains of rock salt and olive oil. Use the pulse button

basilico

or flick the 'on' button intermittently. Little by little as the basil is being finely chopped, transfer it to the container with the pine nuts. Fold in the quark and add enough oil to cover the *pesto* completely. The grated cheese can be added right at the last minute when you dress the hot pasta with the *pesto*. This pesto will keep in the fridge for a few days as it is covered with oil.

Serves 10 with 1kg of pasta.

Until twenty years ago, the port of Santa Margherita was predominantly a fisherman's port and wasn't particularly well equipped for tourist craft. Nonetheless, for two years running my father rented a mooring there for our boat *Endless*. The name had been chosen at the end of an exhausting evening in Milan, when the whole family had been gathered around the table after dinner in a vain attempt to find a name that everyone liked. My father drowsily suggested that we leave it without a name, and my mother with her excellent grasp of the English language after her years spent in London, suggested 'nameless'. I got the job of looking it up in the dictionary to check its spelling, but another word with the suffix '-less' jumped up at me from the page: 'endless'. My parents started to sing a song together, one I had never heard, a composition of Gino Paoli's, a *cantautore* from Genoa. *Cantautori* are poets who set their poems to music.

SENZA FINE[6]
Tu sei un attimo senza fine, non hai oggi non hai domani
non m'importa della luna, non m'importa delle stelle
tu per me sei luna e stelle .
tu per me sei sole e cielo
tu per me sei tutto quanto voglio avere . . . senza fine.

---

6   Gino Paoli, 1961.

ENDLESS

You are a moment without end, you have no todays and no tomorrows
I don't care about the moon, I don't care about the stars
You are the moon and stars for me
You are the sun and the sky for me
You are everything I want . . . endlessly.

Every time that I hear the song now I relive that happy evening spent around the table with my family. And whenever I say the word 'endless' with a certain emphasis, the song comes to mind.

The *Endless* was one of the few pleasure boats in the tiny port of Santa. My father would say that he had been constrained to change from Forte Dei Marmi to Santa Margherita because of one of his daughter's crushes. He was referring to me! I really don't believe that this was the determining factor in the choice of where we would spend our summer holidays, but it is true that my first crush, a certain Dario, also had a holiday house at Rapallo, 4km away from Santa Margherita.

My father loved boats because they fuelled his passion for things mechanical. As I have noted, he was always the only one that never had a tan. When we were anchored, or moored at the quay, we would amuse ourselves between taking dips in the sea and sunbathing on the fly deck, while he would be in the bilge room with the engines. At that time my sister Giudi was eight and not unlike a German shepherd, who while still puppies have funny long legs out of proportion with the rest of their bodies. She was really skinny with two toothpicks for legs. Giudi and I formed a coalition with my mother to try to get my father out of the bilges and make him take the boat out of the port. For anyone who enjoys spending the holidays on a boat, the Golfo di Tigullio is the perfect place. It is wide, bordered at the north by the Monte di Portofino and on the south by Moneglia. Within a few nautical miles you will find many enchanting spots which are still accessible only by sea.

Before departing for our daily trip, we would always check that we had enough provisions. Liguria seems to have ideal food for picnics. The most versatile, available in any bakery, is the famous *focaccia* of Genoa, flat and oozing with fragrant olive oil. They come in different versions: plain, with onions, with olives or with cheese. Then there is the *castagnaccio*, an unusual cake because it has no added sugar but is made with flour, water, olive oil and raisins and seasoned with herbs according to individual taste or as family recipes dictate – fennel seeds, laurel or rosemary. One of the most original local specialities must be the *farinata*. It has a surprising taste and an extremely high nutritional value because it is made with chickpea flour and is therefore rich in vegetable proteins and olive oil. Really easy to make, even at home, it just needs to be left to rise for a reasonable length of time. It was traditionally prepared as an alternative to fish on Fridays, a meatless day for practising Catholics. Today it is still cooked on a baking tray of soldered copper with 3–4cm sides. This takes ten minutes in a wood-fired oven which reaches a temperature of 300°C.

FARINATA

With my home oven I use a 40cm diameter oven pan to accommodate a batter made with 300g of chickpea flour and a litre of warm water.

Pour the water into a bowl and gradually mix in the flour, adding salt to taste. Bear in mind that it always seems more insipid when uncooked. When there are no more lumps, leave the mixture to rest covered with clingfilm for 4 hours at room temperature.

Remove the foam which has formed on top and add 4 tablespoons of extra virgin olive oil then pour the batter into the oven pan to less than a centimetre in height. Bake it in a very hot oven – 250°C – until the surface has formed a hazelnut-coloured film. Internally the *farinata* should be still soft. It takes 30–40 minutes.

Remove from the oven, sprinkle with rosemary needles, freshly ground pepper and oil, and serve hot.

One of our favourite destinations was the small seaside village of Riva Trigoso, located just south of Sestri Levante, where the Golfo di Tigullio ends, and to the north of Cinque Terre. The landscape is completely different here. The coast becomes rocky and juts out over the sea while the sea bottom is also rocky and it seems like you are being submerged in huge blue pools.

Here you find numerous bays accessible by boat or by foot. At the end of one of those lazy summer days, after lots of swims and just as many showers in cold water followed by my father's shouts of displeasure because in those days I couldn't stand the very thing which I now adore, the feeling of salt water on my skin, we had stopped in Riva Trigoso on the very day of the festival known as the Sagra del Bagnun, in mid July. The *bagnun* (a dialect word for *bagno* meaning both swim and bath and in its different dialect forms also meaning sauce) is a kind of 'blue' fish soup, made with the cheaper and less popular fish such as fresh anchovies, together with onion, garlic, parsley, tomato, wine and water, cooked in an earthenware pot and eaten with slices of dried bread called *gallette*.

On feast days the *bagnun* is prepared on the beach in huge pots where it simmers for hours, spreading its aroma all around. But the thing that makes it really special is the addition of aromatic herbs that are found in the inaccessible hills sheer above the sea. Here the fragrances are intense and the few gusts of wind carry different smells at different hours of the day and depending on the wind direction.

A light sea breeze had risen at sunset, but it was still hot as it always is in July at the seaside and we were all still in our swim-suits on the beach in front of the huge pot giving off an intense aroma of the sea. My father was talking to one of the fishermen who seemed ancient to me because of the deep wrinkles that furrowed his dark brown skin. He was telling my father how the recipe originated from the need to provide the fishermen with fresh food using readily available ingredients. In the past the fishermen would prepare it at dawn when they returned from their nocturnal fishing expeditions, on tiny coal stoves they had installed on their boats in order to be able to make themselves a coffee during the night, and they would eat the *bagnun* for breakfast while they waited for their nets to dry in the sun.

In autumn when there wasn't yet any snow on the mountains we would go to the seaside for the weekend. It is the best season for visiting those spots that are usually full of tourists, like San Fruttuoso, where there is a 13th century abbey and a square tower built in the 16th century in order to protect the hamlet from Turkish invasions.

On my first visit to the abbey it was in grave state of disrepair. But in 1986 it was restored to its former glory. The *borgo* is particularly enchanting at night, when everything becomes silent again and the abbey and the tower are illuminated by a pale yellow light suffusing the surrounds with a magical atmosphere. It is at this time that you can believe the legend that recounts the origins of the hermitage that was to become the imposing abbey. In the 3rd century AD a terrible storm hurled five priests onto these shores, which were guarded by a dragon. But one of God's angels defeated the dragon and led the exhausted priests to the spring of clear, cool water that still exists to this day.

The tiny *borgo*, which consists of only 20 inhabitants but boasts four restaurants, is situated between Portofino and Camogli on the slopes of a very steep gorge of the Monte di Portofino and is reached only by sea or on foot by following the route that goes from Nozarego to Paraggi and to Portofino. From the beginning of spring to the end of summer, the beach, a strip of land seventy metres long and less than twenty metres wide which came into existence only after a flood at the beginning of the century, is completely overrun by tourists who disembark from the boats coming from Camogli. When it was clear that we weren't going to be able to moor the boat in the tiny cove, my father organised for us to get there in the rubber dinghy. The plan was to dive to be able to see the statue of Christ that is visible a few metres underwater near the shore. The idea didn't appeal to me in the slightest, because I become seized by panic when I am confronted by inanimate objects underwater, whether they be statues, the piles of a wharf or even the chains attached to buoys. There is probably a psychological explanation that a couple of sessions with a good therapist would uncover, but I prefer to accept this state of affairs and limit myself to looking at these objects in photographs. As it was too cold that day anyway, even for a quick dip, and the water was too rough to be able to see the depths, we opted to go for a walk on dry land.

In the early afternoon the wind began to get stronger and the sea rougher, so much so that my father decided that Giudi, my mother and I should make the return trip by ferry. He would return in the rubber dinghy having secured it with a towrope to the ferry. When we had only just passed the Cape of Portofino, the waves became so huge that my father and the dinghy would disappear behind a wall of water, still connected by means of the towrope.

In spite of the sprays of water that completely drenched us, Giudi and I remained at the stern for the whole crossing, silently watching my father who at regular intervals would appear on the crest of a wave only to disappear behind the next one.

CHAPTER EIGHT

The perfume of flowers

June is my favourite month in Italy, when summer explodes, the days are long and school is about to finish. The colour and fragrance of flowers surrounds you. Maybe I love it because it's the month when I was born, or maybe it's because it's when *zia* Luciana's house at Dagnente is abuzz with endless celebrations and food.

Dagnente is a tiny outlying hamlet of Arona, a small tourist town on the Piedmontese banks of Lago Maggiore. Sited defensively 200 metres above the lake, it hasn't changed much since I was a child. In those days there were enough children to keep a kindergarten in business, but not today. The few you come across are most likely to be offspring of the summer holidaymakers.

The huge green entrance gate to the villa, flanked by two square pillars crowned by flower-filled urns, is located on the road that rises up towards Dagnente. The villa was originally a

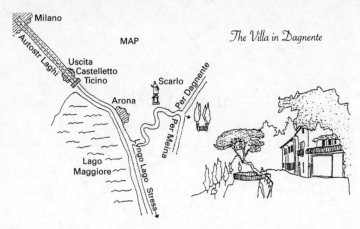

convent, and as is often the case with places designed for peace and meditation, had also been built in a panoramic position, with an eight-hectare park. Tall pine trees planted by *zio* Piero, *zia* Luciana's husband, whose family owned the villa, border the long driveway of white gravel that came from the riverbanks of the nearby valleys of Ossola. At the end of the driveway the road forks; on the left beyond the house which used to belong to the caretakers and is now a separate dwelling, are marble steps, bordered with hydrangeas that lead to what has been for years *zia* Luciana's house.

Beyond the villa complex, the gravel road comes to an end and here there are lots of rose bushes and the big scarlet maple tree that has always featured in my memories of the place. Here, two grassy paths begin: one leads to a large lawn, now used as a small soccer field, which gently winds its way uphill between earthenware urns and passes beneath the amphitheatre with its panoramic view and Greek statues and the penetrating fragrance of the oregano plants that grow wild between the old stones of the steps. The other path descends beyond what used to be the old vineyard, until it reaches the grove of multicoloured hydrangeas where there is a clearing with chestnut trees and a second entrance to the villa from the road which leads to Meina on the lake shores.

As a child, this was my adventure playground along with my cousins, all boys: Luca, who was the same age as me, his brother Eduardo, two years older, and Matteo, two years younger than me. After a few vain attempts at getting them to play with dolls, I chose instead to learn how to play football, catch lizards by the tail, and of course, climb trees.

Overlooking the external walls of the villa there is a semi-circular lookout tower, paved in grey stone, also from the Ossola valleys and flecked with silver that glitters in the sunlight. Here you come across a large crooked umbrella pine, which from time to time drops its pine cones with their perfumed resin, containing the most delicious pine nuts in the world. The four of us, and occasionally other friends – always boys – couldn't wait for the pine cones to drop by themselves. We would take turns at climbing up to get them, sticky and often still closed as they were. It was a fantastic pastime and had all the elements of a great game: the danger that accompanied the tree climbing, because the branches of the pine go straight up, making it more difficult, and the spirit

The crooked pine

of friendship that was fostered by our need to help each other overcome the danger. Once we had descended from the tree we would hide ourselves in the long grass and in a silence interrupted only by the buzz of the bees and our jaws working overtime, we would satisfy our senses as we savoured our hard-earned treasure.

Nespole – loquats – are among the first summer fruits. The best are the very small ones which are just about all stone surrounded by only a small amount of juicy flesh. Eating them is a ritual. They have to be peeled because the skin is hard, but it's no easy task and it leaves your nails black. And one *nespola* is never enough; they are like cherries in this respect.

In the middle of summer fruit was abundant: there were peaches

Matteo, Eduardo,
Luca and me
(striped trousers)
with Daniela.

and apricots from old but low trees grouped together in a small orchard on a sloping plot of land. I was particularly partial to the red and white currants that grew on the trees of an adjoining property. I would pick them from the few branches that hung over the fence into the grounds of the villa and eat them with great pleasure. The end of July was when the pine nuts were ready. Antonio, the villa's caretaker, had made us a special hammer for extracting the nuts from their cones with minimal damage to the nut; it had a handle and 'head' made of wood.

At the end of August we would climb the young fig tree and gather the green fruit with its sweet, dripping flesh – stolen from the birds that were waiting to feed on it. In October, there were chestnuts on the large tree near the the 'Lake of Vipers' and we would extract them with care from their prickly casings, where they lay side by side snugly fitted together in a perfect embrace. And last but not least there were *cachi* or persimmons, the last fruit before the winter frosts arrived. A certain variety known as 'vanilla' persimmons, characterised by the presence of a stone, are eaten only when they are really soft, and we used to call the process of eating these soft persimmons *la cacata*.[1]

The vineyard had been removed a few years earlier and I can no longer recall the taste of the grapes, but I still remember *ʒio* Piero standing near a stump at the end of a row, under the fading summer sun. I watched him from the path above that led to the weeping willow where we would meet every morning. He is holding a bunch of grapes hanging from a piece of vine shoot and something in his manner tells me that he is sad.

At that time the big house had not yet been divided up among the family, and *nonna* Maria, stern and deaf, who terrified us children, was still alive. From the ground floor, where there was a huge living room furnished with antiques and a country kitchen with its cast-iron cooker and two grey marble sinks, a staircase of

---

1 In vulgar terms – shit, crap.

*My father in nonna Tina's arms with the rest of the household. Lina's
wearing the polka dot dress and Antonio is in the front on the right.*

low steps also made of stone from the nearby valleys, led to the
second floor, divided into two wings. In one wing were the
bedrooms with wardrobes inhabited by noisy woodworms, and
high beds with mattresses that you would be swallowed up by,
supported by a system of wire bedsprings which served as the
trampolines of my youth. The windows were shuttered externally
and secured on the inside by lateral hooks with a horizontal rod
through them. We would have so much fun when we got sick.
When we were all covered in red spots we were put to bed together
in order for us all to contract everything just once and at the same
time. No one has ever been able to explain why I never caught
Matteo's German measles or mumps! The same fate befell my sister
Giudi, who was the same age as Matteo's sister, Marta. I have to
say that those two girls caused more trouble than the boys and I
ever did. They were responsible for infecting the whole tribe of us
with head lice and were in and out of Accident and Emergency at
the hospital. Even now, we can't get them to tell us which of them

swallowed the greatest number of children's aspirins. To be on the safe side both of them had to undergo the torture of having their stomachs pumped.

After *nonna* Maria died, the house began to be divided up, first among the aunts and uncles and then among the existing four grandchildren. During the summer, *nonna* Tina was usually accommodated in the small apartment on the top floor of the house that had belonged to the old caretakers, Lina and Antonio. In the garden opposite there was a small henhouse that I would visit on a daily basis to satisfy my taste for eggs, and a vegetable garden where my knowledge of how to grow plants and vegetables first began.

parsley

A long stairway completely covered by a pergola of perfumed wisteria led to my grandmother's small dwelling, which was composed of just one big room and a bathroom. There was also an old cast-iron stove there, which served additionally as a heater, a large and comfortable armchair and French doors that opened out onto a small terrace, all of which remains exactly the same today, even though the whole house has been completely restructured. When I would return for lunch, outside the front door on a stone table, I would always find one or more wicker baskets full of freshly picked fruit and vegetables. You always knew when a basket contained parsley because its sweet fragrance would waft towards you as you climbed the stairs, and I knew then that I would be spending an hour with my grandmother separating the parsley leaves from the long and delicate stalks, while she would tell me one of her fairytales, nearly all in dialect, which I confess with great regret to having

dandelion

completely forgotten. The parsley leaves are used for the s*alsa verde*, while she sometimes used the stalks to make *riso e prezzemolo* – rice with parsley.

Salsa verde is a recipe found with numerous variations in many parts of Italy. In Piedmont, it is served as an accompaniment for *bollito misto*, a mixture of boiled meats cooked in such an artful manner that the dish has a balanced but surprising taste. In cases like this, anchovies are also found in the *salsa*, which is faithful to the culinary tradition of the region combining meat with fish, its most famous example being *vitello tonnato*, or as it is called in dialect, *Vitel Toné*. With this speciality the veal is marinated in wine, vegetables and aromatic herbs and then braised at length and, once cold, finely sliced and covered with a sauce made with mayonnaise, tuna, capers and anchovies. This is the most well-known version of the dish, but the one I prefer is an old recipe, and calls for the anchovies to be inserted into the meat so that their flavour is released during the cooking process, giving it a more distinct flavour. Just before the meat has finished cooking, the tuna and capers are added to the sauce, which should have reached a reasonably dense and aromatic consistency.

My recipe for *salsa verde* is quick to make and keeps for a reasonable length of time because of the vinegar. In a blender, I blend the leaves of a small bunch of parsley with a few grains of coarse salt, good olive oil, a spoonful of capers and the soft part of a small white bread roll that has been soaked in good wine vinegar, red or white, it doesn't matter, then squeezed dry. I check whether there is enough salt and transfer it to a jar covered with oil until I want to use it. When I am about to serve it I add a hard-boiled egg, finely sliced and, in summer, I stuff fresh tomatoes with the resulting mixture as an apéritif.

To make *riso e prezzemolo* for just the two of us, my grandmother would measure half a cup of rice that she would wash carefully until the water she rinsed it in ran clear, then cook it on a low heat with a cup of water and the parsley stalks. The rice would cook in such a way that the starch was released and the parsley would add a light green creamy texture to the rice. Then she would remove the stalks and add a spoonful of minced parsley leaves and a knob of butter.

il paiolo

Lina and Antonio lived on the ground floor with their two sons, Aldo and Luciano. I cherish the memory of the smell of the hearth of that house, the wood that burned there and the image of the huge copper pot, blackened by the fire and hung over the fireplace, where partly scorched lumps of wood protruded out of the big pile of ash which would be scattered about in the air whenever the small front door was opened.

On the floor of small black tiles with tiny white geometric designs there would be a pile of dry wood to burn, with its own particular sweetish smell of resin. These smells clung to my clothes until my grandmother would wash them and then they would perfume the air anew in this small part of the world that I always carry with me.

Antonio always had a cigarette butt between his lips, a faded straw hat on his head and a scythe and rake in his hands. Lina was short and petite, with her grey hair gathered into a bun and a pannier on her shoulders. Her slightly graceless but soft voice is one I can still hear, as she calls us to come and feed the rabbits or check if the hens have laid, or as she yells at us angrily because we have climbed the tall ladder above the barn again.

At the entrance to the barn there was a fountain of spring water that my mother would use to keep the large watermelons fresh – she always managed to choose them sweet and ripe to just the right degree. She says that if they are sweet they 'sing', because when you hit them with your knuckles they produce a low and melodic sound. In Milan she would go to the market on her bicycle and return home cycling dangerously between the cars, the loose paving stones that many of Milan's streets are still paved with, and the tram tracks, with her many plastic bags hanging off the handlebars. And in the basket attached to the rear parcel rack would be the biggest watermelon that the market had to offer.

The spacious grassy plain where the soccer field was sited ends with a tall bush trimmed in such a way as to create arches under which stone benches have been placed. Beyond this handy shelter from the heat you come across the swimming pool. The small blue tiles that once clad the bottom and the sides of the pool have been covered with a special waterproof material, which among other things retains the heat generated by the all-day sun, making the water a pleasant temperature. Around the edge of the porous white stone of the pool are huge red terracotta slabs, perfect for drying off under the summer sun, and the lawn with four palm trees harbouring amphibious and stinging insects, who are immune to the chlorine and invade the water at the end of summer. On the other side of the pool is a dense pergola supporting a climber with tiny leaves, whose top has been artistic-ally shaped into an arch, with the ample space beneath paved and used to shelter from the sun and glare. The pool cabanas, equipped with hot water for some years now, complete the pool complex.

The pool has always been the meeting place for our extended family in summer. We take turns in peer groups according to informal shifts. In the morning there are the hordes of kids who jump into the pool continuously, trying to empty it of as much water as possible. Then come the teenagers who have risen late and turn up for a swim before lunch, followed by the women trying to substitute lunch with a few hours of swimming, sunbathing and chatting. Covered with foul-smelling mud packs they wander about by the pool, unconcerned that they can be seen from the terrace of the bar l'Arca di Noe'. In any case, in that state they are unrecognisable. In the afternoon the children return and then the teenagers after their tennis game; in the evening it's the turn of the men who don't sunbathe, don't watch their weight, don't wear face masks, don't want to chat and desire nothing more than to read the paper in peace. At different times we all found ourselves in each of these situations.

Taking a different path that slopes down away from the pool, you pass by the old tennis court, where I tried in vain for many years to learn how to play, in the end deciding to restrict myself to watching my sister Giudi and her friends, as I sat on the stone bench near the small arbour. This was the perfect place to sit and read, with just the gentle breeze for company that from May to the beginning of June carries the scent of the mimosa nearby. If it was spring, no matter which part of the villa I found myself in, I could identify where I was just by sniffing the air, heavy with the fragrance of flowers. Every corner of the park had its own distinct perfume.

Just walking across the lawns is relaxing and good for body and soul, but to go collecting wild herbs, rich in vitamins and healing properties, is also an honest-to-goodness ritual that my mother introduced us to when we were children. I have probably always taken for granted her profound knowledge of herbs, dating from her childhood in Valsassina and combined with personal experimentation that has so far had the adverse effect of just one sore stomach, the result of excessive consumption

nettle

of *malva rotundifolia* – common mallow, an excellent laxative. I can recognise the well-known *taraxacum officinalis* or dandelion, often identified by its common names of: *dente di leone*,[2] *dente di cane*,[3] *pisciacane*[4] and *piscialetto*,[5] which all emphasise its diuretic properties, ideal for cleansing the body of toxins after the lethargy of the winter months; the wild asparagus *phytolacca decandra* and the tender *verʒit* or *silene infilata*, whose young leaves are eaten as soon as they sprout. The latter is one of the first herbs to appear at the beginning of March and has an unmistakable taste.

But what interests me the most is the use of flowers in cooking, which is more common than you might think, if we take into account that the caper and the common cauliflower are, as the name itself suggests, flowers.

primrose

The humble primrose or *primula vulgaris*, growing timidly when nature is still drowsy from under foliage rotted by the water and snow, is excellent in salads with flakes of Parmesan. And still to come is *portulaca oleracea* – portulaca, rich in vitamin A, perfect in tomato and onion salad, with the addition of a spoonful of daisy petals.

Frittelle, deep-fried flowers, have always featured in Italian cooking: pumpkin flowers, dipped in a batter and perhaps with a piece of *mozzarella* and anchovy, or *sambuco* – elderflowers, whose berries are used to make an interesting jam and a laxative syrup at the end of August, which in our house we used to call *caghereccio*.

Using rose petals that are always available you can make a variation of *crème caramel* by adding the petals of two broken roses to the cold milk together with a tablespoon of cognac and one of sherry.

2   Lion's tooth.
3   Dog's tooth.
4   Pissing dog.
5   Bed wetter.

The weekends at Dagnente are often a good opportunity for relaxing, reading and playing a bit of sport, just enough to justify the gargantuan meals. The only diversion is going to do the shopping 'in town', that is, in Arona. The road that winds down into the centre of Arona passes beneath the copper statue of San Carlo Borromeo, better known as the Sancarlone. It is a huge statue, built at the end of the 1600s, more than 23 metres high and resting on a pedestal of 12 metres which, according to local imagination, inspired the creators of the Statue of Liberty, some 200 years later. Up until just a few years ago it was possible to climb the statue right up to its head, via an internal stairwell, an absolute nightmare for claustrophobics. At the top you were met by a fantastic view of the lake as well as an impressive view of San Carlone's aquiline nose, a good half metre long. The statue isn't aesthetically pleasing, but it serves as a tourist attraction, as borne out by the dozens of tour buses that deposit their visitors in the *piazza* facing it.

Past the Sancarlone, the road curves and drops steeply towards the lake, passing the votive chapels scattered among the hills until it reaches a small statue of the Madonna. It is customary to give a little toot when passing. Through the dense vegetation you can start to make out the lake and the sunny banks of Angera overlooking Arona.

We usually bought our bread, together with a piece of *focaccia* at the *panificio* or bakery in the Corso Cavour, with its clothes shops and the Pasticceria Aliverti, famous for its *meringata*, a cake made of meringue, candied chestnuts and flakes of chocolate, a real dieter's nightmare. A few years ago they introduced a summer version, which replaces the chestnuts with wild strawberries and dark chocolate with white. The calorie count doesn't change all that much, but the colours are definitely more evocative of summer and it goes some way towards alleviating one's sense of guilt. After all, respecting the seasonality of food is part of healthy eating habits.

They say that the lake is sad when the sun is absent, but not for those who are able to experience its different moods, like the magic of the still water only gently disturbed by the swans that appear suspended on its surface, on mornings when the mist hasn't yet lifted.

With its autumnal warmth, the sun accompanies those who enjoy walking by the lakeside and allow themselves to be beguiled by the surrounding tranquillity, while stopping to look at the statue of the boatman, pipe in his mouth, whose gaze seems to lose itself beyond the horizon, beyond the Lombard shore which is so close, and beyond the hills where the lakes of Varese, Monate and Comabbio are found.

The lakeside comes to an end under a pergola of lilac wisteria that flowers from spring to the end of summer and which then flowers later and for a shorter period of time with white, intensely perfumed, smaller blooms.

The road curves abruptly and at the corner, sheer above the sea, is the Bar Il Cantuccio and, next door to it, the Taverna del Pittore, a restaurant which you can also reach from the water, mooring your motorboat at a private jetty.

The summer I was born, my father had bought a beautiful Riva Tritone, a kind of wooden speedboat popular in the 1950s and 60s that he used to take my mother water skiing, unperturbed by the fact that she was still breastfeeding me! They would anchor in this spot that we would subsequently return to many times over the years, except then we would enter by means of the *piazza*. We would book one of the tables on the terrace where you could either enjoy the fresh air or be exposed to the damp, according to the opposing views of my father and mother respectively. I was used to their lighthearted banter and in the meantime would watch the swans below and enjoy my favourite dish, which is still on the menu at the restaurant today: *pesce persico al burro e risotto bianco* – poached perch in butter with white risotto.

On Sundays Arona is invaded by tourists, mostly from Milan, in search of an 'outing in the fresh air' – or, more accurately, an 'outing stuck in a traffic jam'. When there isn't heavy traffic, it takes an hour to get from our house in Milan to the Chiosco del Cammillo – Cammillo's Kiosk, which makes the best vanilla ice-cream in the area – following the motorway which goes to the lakes in the direction of Switzerland, and on clear days enjoying the spectacular view of the Alps, especially Mt Rosa, second only to Mt Blanc among the highest peaks in Europe, and so named because of the intense colour it turns at sunset.

It's impossible to do the trip north in less than three hours, while the evening return trip is, despite the existence today of the motorway, an uninterrupted column of cars which winds it way from Stresa, the most touristy part of the whole shoreline of Lake Maggiore, right up to the toll gates at the entrance to Milan.

There was a party for my eighteenth birthday, and the weather was perfect for it. My *zia* Luciana has always had a real talent and fabulous taste when it comes to throwing parties. She is not the least perturbed at the thought of having fifty or more guests. For my eighteenth birthday she chose a rustic theme.

Under the portico that she had had built over the front door, my aunt had laid a long table for a buffet, with three different red-and-white checked tablecloths. In the middle of the table on two huge wooden chopping blocks, cheeses and salami were beautifully displayed.

There was the big round fatty goose salami, surrounded by tiny *cacciatorini* and next to them, partially sliced, was the long and square-shaped *salsiccia passita*, alongside a well-known speciality of the Abruzzo region with the vulgar name of *i coglioni di mulo* – mule's balls, because they are two rounds of salami tied together. There was also *le tome di montagna* (mountain cheeses) such as the *bettelmat* from the Val d'Ossola, with its characteristic flavour of *mottolina*, a common herb found in these valleys, and the more mature *spress* from the Valle Fromazza. Next to the two chopping boards there are two wicker baskets lined with red napkins, overflowing with sticks of *pane casereccio*, cut into pieces, and *focacce* of the plainest type, either dripping with olive oil or with onion, cut into long thin slices.

My cousin Daniela had helped me to choose something to wear from her ample wardrobe. The long full skirt with a petticoat of tiny lace, white and made of panels each with a different scene, embroidered by hand and all sown together, gave me a vaguely peasant-like appearance. Over a plain white t-shirt, we added a waistcoat of antique lace that could only be worn to welcome the guests, after which I had to return it respectfully to the trunk of family mementos. There was no need to police this, because less than an hour after everyone had arrived we were all headed for the pool in our swimsuits and with our tennis rackets.

My aunt had also organised lots of surprises for my party, starting when she came up to the pool with Lina, carrying baskets filled with cold drinks and *gnocco fritto*, a speciality of Modena which I adore, perfect with salami, but which I prefer to eat on its own.

GNOCCO FRITTO

A mid-morning meal for peasant farmers who began their day well before dawn, *il gnocco fritto*, is a substitute for bread.

500g plain flour
70g oil (or lard)
250ml water
1 teaspoon baking soda
1 teaspoon salt
olive oil

Incorporate the flour, oil and water (into which baking soda and salt have been previously mixed), or use milk, which gives a more soft and elastic *gnocco*. Knead dough until firm and elastic (with a texture more like *pasta fresca*, rather than bread dough).

Leave to rest for at least half an hour, then roll out into a thin sheet. Cut into diamond shapes and fry in a pot of oil. They will puff up immediately as soon as they touch the oil. Drain, then serve with vegetables, salami and cheese.

When we got back from the pool, brightly coloured ceramic platters had appeared with the freshest *mozzarella* and red and yellow roasted peppers, seasoned with garlic, oil and capers. To make this dish you should choose the plumpest peppers that are then seared over the flame of the gas stove until they blacken. If you put them into a paper bag afterwards the skins lift off more easily, then you slice them into layers. For me, searing peppers has a special meaning, I feel like I am enacting my family's rituals. Even today, despite the fact that the barbecue is an adequate substitute for this method, I still prefer to stand in front of the gas stove and slowly, using my hands, rotate the pepper over the flame until it has become completely black. The aroma that fills the kitchen evokes happy memories and makes the labour of the successive cleaning required worthwhile.

My aunt's pâté, a unique recipe that has been handed down to the whole family and jealously guarded, had also been put on the table. There were colourful pasta salads and, essential for completing the composition of this rustic feast, *pasta e fagioli*, pasta and beans, served cold in a rough earthenware soup tureen. For this dish to be made correctly, it should have such a thick consistency that the spoon can stand upright in the middle of it. And to finish, there was a multicoloured array of fruit and desserts: strawberries, raspberries, redcurrants and apricots, to accompany the *gelato* from Camillo's, and peaches filled with *amaretti*, a particular Modenese tradition.

AMARETTI PEACHES

1/2 cup coarsely chopped *amaretti* biscuits
2 tablespoons sugar (vary amount according to taste)
3–4 tablespoons cocoa
1/2 glass *amaretto* liqueur
6 large peaches or nectarines, halved
pine nuts as decoration

Put crushed biscuits in bowl together with sugar and cocoa powder a little at a time, until the right consistency is reached. Add a few drops of *amaretto* if mixture is too dry.

Cut peaches in half through natural indentations, twist, pull apart, and remove stones (cut them out if necessary). Sprinkle with a little sugar if peaches seem a bit tart.

Put peaches in a shallow baking dish, cut side up. Spoon biscuit mixture into the cavity of each peach, using up all mixture. Decorate with pine nuts.

Pour over *amaretto* (you can add more at this stage or partway through cooking as it tends to evaporate, and the syrupy juice is great to spoon over when finished). Bake in oven preheated to 180° for 20–30 minutes.

Serve warm or cold.

Zia Luciana's porch was our favourite study spot, even during our university years, first for me and then for Giudi and Marta. It was always cool, even in the hottest part of the day, and to reinvigorate yourself all you had to do was look up and let your thoughts wander to the huge white flowers of the old magnolia tree in front of you, or just beyond it where you could see part of the lake, the tip of Ranco. Involuntarily your mouth would begin to water at the thought of Il Sole restaurant at Ranco, one of the most successful restaurants in Italy. For me, studying and eating have always been intimately related. I have tried hundreds of substitutes, from herbal teas to carob chocolate, without finding any satisfaction, until I discovered that cooking, with its accompanying requirement of trying what you have made, works well to fulfil this need, and at least other people benefit. The silence is absolute, except for the sounds that will always be synonymous with those peaceful and solitary hours spent on the porch: the buzz of the bees, intent on devouring the nectar of the white jasmine which covered part of the wall around the French door which led to the kitchen; the sighs of Black, the caretaker's dog, who with a dull thud would plop himself down between your legs; the current caretaker's footsteps, Gianni's hurried ones or Lucia's softer ones, on the gravel that covers the path between the porch and the house.

In June, the year after my eighteenth birthday, Miki, my school-mate for eight years and still my best friend, studied with me at *zia* Luciana's house for our school-leaving exams. On the agenda was study from 6–9 a.m., jogging and a swim in the pool, breakfast at the café, study 11–2 p.m., a break, then study till 7 p.m. and the evening off. This was all carefully recorded in writing, divided up over the fourteen days preceding the exam, including revision and a mock exam.

As it turned out we passed, we took lots of breaks, but we hardly ever followed the study timetable. And that wasn't necessarily our fault; there was always someone who would pop in to see us, sometimes with alternative plans that we were unable to turn down.

Stefano, whom we nicknamed *pisello* or pea, because it was the colour of his classic Citroen 2CV, had a motorboat that was perfect for lake excursions. One memorable adventure was our visit to the hermitage of Santa Caterina del Sasso. It's an impressive architectural complex set in the rock face of Sasso Ballaro, a mountain that rises sheer above the lake from a point where the water is more than 200 metres deep.

According to a 3rd century legend, the rich merchant Alberto Besozzi, returning from a profitable business venture at the Lesa market, a small town on the Piedmontese shores of the lake, was saved from certain shipwreck by asking for help from Santa Caterina D'Alessandria, offering in return to convert to the faith. He spent the rest of his life in a cave and traces still remain there today. When there was a plague, as a result of his prayers the inhabitants of the lake received God's mercy and in thanks they built a tiny church on this rock spur, dedicated to Santa Caterina. That day marked the start of the construction of the whole complex, composed today of a church which conserves the traces of three previous constructions and the grotto where Besozzi took refuge, a tiny gothic convent and a group of buildings which sprung up in the 1300s and were subsequently rearranged.

Depending on the light at different hours of the day, this complex built on a strip of incredibly narrow land seems to be part of the rock behind it. The easiest way of getting there is by means of the lake, and it is also the most spectacular. From the wharf looking up, you can't see the hermitage, only the impressive wall of rock that sticks out like a threatening canopy above you. A Benedictine monk of the order of S. Benedetto da Norcia, with his mighty belly and cream tunic with wide sleeves and a hood which covered his head to the point of obscuring his eyes, told us off for making such a racket and invited to us complete our visit with haste.

Other places of interest not to be missed in this area are the Borromee Islands: Isola dei Pescatori or Fisherman's Island, Isola Bella, the Beautiful Island, and Isola Madre, the Mother Island. There is an ornate baroque palace with landscaped gardens on Isola Bella. Isola Madre is the largest of the three islands, which I have only ever admired from the lake, and is famous for its enormous botanic garden and its petulant white peacocks. My favourite will always be Isola dei Pescatori, 350 metres long and only 100 metres wide and at its most magnificent when it is cloaked in snow. In the early hours of the morning, on those rare winter days when the sun puts in an appearance and the mist has only just lifted from the lake, the island appears to be a raft, leisurely transporting those small houses, all of them painted white, except for the very last one which is pink. This is the Hotel Verbano, built on the point that juts out towards Isola Bella. Two romantic rooms look out onto a rock face covered with plants and shrubs that emerges in the small strait between the Isola dei Pescatori and Isola Bella and which popular imagination has given the name Isola degli Innamorati – Lovers' Island.

GLOSSARY:

BETTELMATT (ba-ttal-maht) is a particularly highly esteemed member of the *toma* family of cheeses from the high pastures of the Val d'Ossola. People say that the special flavour of the valley's cheeses comes from a herb known as *mottolina* that grows only in Val d'Ossola. But it is the overall quality of the grazing that gives Bettelmatt its unique taste profile. Produced only in the summer months, Bettelmatt's cheese-making technique resembles that used for Gruyère. Whole raw milk is heated to 36–40°C in copper vats and coagulated for 25–30 minutes. The soft curd is then cut into pea-sized granules, left to stand for a short time, and cooked. The curd deposits on the bottom of the vat and is then gathered up in a cloth and placed in hoops. After cooling, the curd is pressed mechanically for 12–24 hours. It then goes into brine for 10–15 days, or may be dry-salted, after which it is left in a cool place to mature for a minimum of two months.

SPRESS (spreh-s) is a cheese whose name derives from the same word, meaning the pressed curd. Once it was a very low-fat cheese as the milk was skimmed several times and dairy farmers were much more interested in obtaining butter than cheese. The modern version, like many mountain Nostrano cheeses, is made from skimmed milk. The milk is heated to 35–36°C, inoculated with powdered rennet, and 25–30 minutes later the curd is cut up into hazelnut-sized lumps. The soft curd is then semi-cooked at 40°C for 30 minutes and left to stand in the whey for a further 40 minutes. It is transferred into moulds, where it is salted in a brine bath for four days. Subsequently the rounds are matured in a cool (8°C) room, where they are turned over and brushed every day.

CHAPTER NINE

Holidays in Sardinia

Viewed from the air, the Emerald Coast was a sight of incomparable splendour – the sea with that hint of green which gives its name to this northern part of the island of Sardinia, the white sand beaches, and Cape Testa, the northernmost point, an expanse of rock sculpted by the sea winds, all created the impression that the island was uninhabited. The island's vegetation was still green in June, but nothing could have prepared me for the fragrant blast that I experienced as I stood at the door of the plane.

It was most definitely much hotter than in Milan, even taking into account the fact that in the 1970s the seasons were more reliable and June on the mainland held the promise of long hot days. The heat given off by the tarmac at the airport of Olbia was exaggerated by the humidity until a cooling sea breeze brought with it a sharp and unexpected fragrance that I could not identify.

In those days the airport was small and quite basic and it didn't

take long for us to retrieve our luggage. My father's was a navy
blue canvas bag with large white handles made out of a reinforced
fabric that was also used as trim, conferring on the bag the desired
seafarer's style. My own suitcase was square and beige, with a
darker trim. My father had bought it for me as a present especially
for this trip to visit my mother, who was taking an intensive sailing
course on the island of Caprera. Giudi was still too small to
accompany us on such a journey.

It was all the rage to learn to sail on this deserted island, which
housed only the spartan sailing school, where the students slept in
mixed dorms on bunk beds with outdoor bathrooms and field
kitchens. They sailed on large, slow yachts for most of the day,
and for the rest of the time prepared meals and cleaned according
to a roster. My father had seized the opportunity to accept the
challenge my mother had issued at the dinner table, that even
though she was 40 years old she still had more energy than her

two daughters. The Caprera sailing school was just the place to prove it.

How she managed to stand it for two weeks is still a mystery. Not because life there was really as hard as all that, but more because my mother's personality was very different from that of the other students. They were for the most part young and un-prejudiced, more interested in getting to know each other than in learning how to sail, whereas my mother had probably decided that she would really apply herself and learn the ropes. Our arrival was most certainly unexpected.

I can remember in detail the trip from the airport to Porto Rotondo because when I returned ten years later, everything had changed. Then, the road was poorly sealed, a thin strip of paving that wound through sparse vegetation of mainly small green shrubs with tiny white flowers. I found it hard to imagine that these tiny white flowers were responsible for the intense fragrance I had noticed earlier. It was the scent of myrtle, a native evergreen bush that manages to grow even in the driest and rockiest of soils. In ancient times it symbolised love and beauty. Legend has it that Venus used myrtle to protect herself from unwanted admirers: in mythological representation, a crown of myrtle adorns her blonde hair. Myrtle was also planted around the temples dedicated to the Goddess of Love, and for many centuries brides would wear sprigs of myrtle in their hair. According to another legend, Adam is said to have given Eve a sprig of myrtle as a love token, receiving an apple in exchange!

My father had booked us into the Sporting Club at Porto Rotondo, at the time the only hotel at Punta Lepre, which is now overrun by cement buildings. The rooms consisted of bungalows with French doors opening straight onto the beachfront, which was really a series of rocks emerging out of a sea of indescribable hue. Each bungalow had a huge basket of fruit that covered the whole of a small table, overflowing with *fichi d'india*, which reminded me of the sweet and juicy ones I had eaten the year before on Vulcano.

In the early morning, before the ever-present wind that blows in Sardinia had risen and the sky was even bluer than the sea, you could easily distinguish all the rock dwellers. There were the polyps that seem to be naturally playful and curious, as they would willingly approach the white handkerchief that my father had lowered into the water. They really did seem entertained by the game of tug of war that we improvised. The red sea anemones were easily detached from the rocks without effort or risk, while the sea urchins with their long thin spikes soon ended up sprinkled with lemon in an impromptu dish prepared by my father, who preferred them to fruit.

During the hottest part of the day, the water is a turquoise colour that can only be compared to the precious stone of the same name. The surface is rippled by a wind which is the only thing that makes it bearable to remain out in the sun. The sea floor is invisible, but it is wonderful to swim underwater because of the rays of the sun filtering down, creating a marvellous play of light. The best time for swimming is at dawn when the wind has dropped, but a light breeze coming from the shore carries the scent of myrtle. Then the colour of the sea becomes darker and merges with the sky and you feel as if you are floating on an endless surface.

My father had organised for us to go to Caprera, one of the islands in the archipelago of the Maddalena Islands, in a motorboat with a fridge full of everything my mother could possibly want: shrimps (but no lobster) and white wine. Caprera, now connected to the island of Maddalena by means of a bridge, boasts white sandy beaches that contrast with the sea, which has a shallow bottom of sand and rock and turns colours which defy the imagination. The names of the bays are evocative of their landscape: Cala Serena,

On the boat to Caprera Island, 1975.

Calm Bay, with its white rocks whose surfaces have been made smooth by the waters, Cala Tahiti with its extraordinarily beautifully coloured waters, as the name suggests, reminiscent of Polynesia.

When we arrived at Cala Baccà where the sailing school run by the Italian Navy League is situated, the boats were already in the water and it was hard to work out which one my mother was on. My father wasted no time in calling out to her on the megaphone and I heard my mother's unmistakable shout of surprise as I began to make her out at the helm of one of the heavy Caravels. The manoeuvre for bringing the boat into shore took longer than my mother could stand, and so letting her enthusiasm get the better of her, she jumped into the water fully clothed. Apparently this was not the first time in the many drills which included capsizing that she had run out of dry clothes.

I can remember clearly the moment she surfaced, with her brown face upturned to the sky and her eyes and mouth shut tight. It had always amazed me how she managed to swim without opening her eyes, firmly convinced that if she should swallow even a drop of water she would drown. When she was sure that she had really made it to the surface she would come out with one of her favourite expressions: 'ecco fatto il becco all'oca' – 'that's that, then'!

After the first five minutes of disbelief came the hugs, or rather 'crushings', which my mother with her strong sense of realism liked to call them, and we decided to have lunch on dry land, where for the most part it was a choice between either the beach full of boats and young people, or the hill with its lookout tower. We made our way up the hill where you can enjoy a spectacular view of the sea and the nearby islands, surrounded by the myrtle bushes which I had come to recognise by now, taking care to avoid the many rabbits which scampered about in the tall grass.

It was a fantastic day and the memory I have of my mother's extreme joy is as strong as that of my father's more low-key pleasure. He had once again succeeded in surprising us – doing whatever it would take to make his 'three women' happy was to be my father's calling in life.

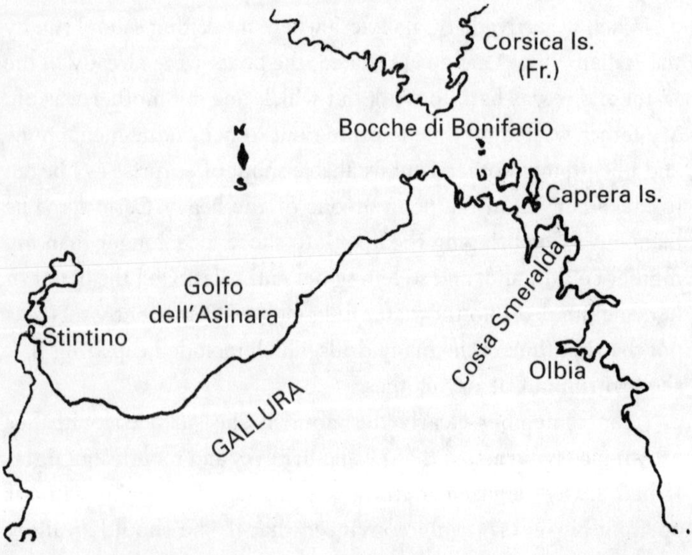

Corsica Is. (Fr.)

Bocche di Bonifacio

Caprera Is.

Golfo dell'Asinara

Costa Smeralda

Stintino

Olbia

GALLURA

It is not easy for a tourist to discover the local cuisine on Sardinia because it is still mainly a traditional and unceremonious one and is linked to the cultivation of the land. But when I tried some of the specialities associated with this place, it felt as if I had been able to penetrate the secrets of an ancient culture.

I will never forget my first dinner invitation, which had been somewhat a result of circumstance. The *Endless* had been moored in the port of Stintino and wasn't particularly well sheltered from the sea, which had been rough for a few days. Stintino rises up on a narrow stretch of land that divides the bay into two coves, nestled in the large Gulf of Asinara. After the third night of rough seas, my mother had pitched camp in the churchyard, quite determined not to get back on board the boat. After a further two days when the fury of the sea had still not abated, there was no other choice than to try and 'outwit the weather'. And this is how we came to make the acquaintance of a few local families and were invited to eat *porceddu* – suckling pig, the jewel in the crown of the cuisine of Sardinia.

The whole pig, which doesn't weigh more than 4kg, is skewered on a spit and roasted slowly for about four hours in a pit with charcoal made from aromatic shrubs such as myrtle, juniper berry and olive. Traditionally the spit itself should be made of strawberry tree wood, an evergreen shrub found in all the hottest parts of the Mediterranean that produces tiny fruit of a distinctive scarlet colour and a sweet and pleasantly woody taste also characteristic of the local honey, which is actually extracted from the strawberry flower.

While the pig is cooking it is greased with *lardo* or bacon fat and when it has nearly finished cooking it is covered with myrtle until it absorbs its scent. The ritual cooking of the pig on the spit is an honour reserved exclusively for men.

Her churchyard protest and the suckling pig are all that my mother remembers of that holiday, partly because she and Giudi chose to make the return trip by ferry as soon as the storm subsided. I courageously chose to stay with my father and face the crossing to the mainland which, contrary to the forecasts, was made on one of those rare days in which the sea was completely flat, even in the notorious Bocche di Bonifacio – the canal which separates the islands of Sardinia and Corsica. Part of the journey involved the stop, obligatory when we were in these parts, at the island of Budelli, where we would swim right up to the Spiaggia Rosa, the Pink Beach famous for the special peach colour of its sand. The phenomenon is a result of the slow decomposition of the granite, which under the combined action of the heat and the salt deposits is mixed with a huge quantity of marine micro-organisms that have been washed up on the shores by the water currents. The sum of colours of this minuscule blend gives the sand its particular hue that isn't actually that easy to see in summer, thanks to the dreadful habit of the tourists who persist in taking away plastic bags full of the sand. The granite on the sea bottom gives the water a crystal clarity and a colour that alternates between a light blue and aquamarine. The island is no more than a kilometre long and is covered with a dense thick blotch of strawberry trees, myrtle, and lentiscus, whose fragrance carried by the wind is a kind of *benvenuto* and *arrivederci* [1] to Sardinia.

Sardinian cooking can be divided into three distinct styles: the cuisine of the sea, a pastoral cuisine, and that of the peasants, with a huge variety of typical Mediterranean fruit and vegetables. Sardinian artichokes are small and spiky, and Sardinian tomatoes, hard and red with green stripes, are unmistakable and considered to be real delicacies with good reason.

Out of the four provinces, you will find all three styles of Sardinian cuisine only in Sassari and Cagliari, the latter being the capital of the island; the zone of Nuoro is strongly characterised by sheep farming and Oristano is a seafaring zone. The cuisine that has evolved from the sea's bounty is used for seafood salads

---

1   Welcome and farewell.

and antipasto. There is lobster cooked in *vernaccia* – a dry white wine, amber yellow in colour with a strongly aromatic bouquet of almond blossoms and produced in Oristano – as well as the *bottarga*, tuna or mullet roe, which is removed immediately after the fish has been caught, salted and dried. While *bottarga* is most commonly found already grated and used to dress pasta, the Sards still prefer to eat it finely sliced and seasoned with oil and lemon.

The pastoral style of cooking is based on substantial first courses including spelt soup; *malloreddus*, small concave shells made out of durum wheat and saffron; and different types of ravioli – *culingiones* and *angiulottus*, served with sheep ragout and cheese, usually *pecorino* in many different varieties, among which Fiore Sardo stands out.

Malloreddus, a dialect term for bobby calf, are also called *gnocchetti sardi*.

MALLOREDDUS WITH SAUSAGE RAGU'

1 onion
1 clove garlic
3 tablespoons extra virgin olive oil
4 fresh basil leaves
200g Italian style sausages (pure pork, coarsely minced)
500g ripe tomatoes
salt and pepper
350g *gnocchetti sardi*
1 sachet saffron powder
4 tablespoons *pecorino* cheese

Finely chop the onion and crush the clove of garlic whole, using the back of a heavy knife.

Heat the oil in a large frypan (large enough to accommodate the pasta later on). Add the garlic, onion, basil and sausage meat (squeeze out of skin) and lightly fry for 3 minutes. Add the peeled, quartered fresh tomatoes and simmer for 15 minutes, then discard the garlic.

In the meantime, in a large saucepan, bring plenty of water to the boil, add salt and cook the pasta until *al dente*. Before draining the pasta, throw away only half the cooking water. Add the saffron powder to this water, stir the pasta gently, then drain.

Transfer the now yellow-tinted pasta to the sausage *ragu'* and serve with a good sprinkle of grated *pecorino* cheese.

The element that all three gastronomic cultures of Sardinia share is bread, the staple food common to all the people of the Mediterranean, but in Sardinia also a symbol of religious and social traditions, associated with the passing of the seasons and the work cycles such as shearing, harvesting and the grape harvest.

On the morning of the last day of the year the children of Orgosolo knock on village doors, and ask for *su cocone*, bread especially prepared for the occasion, along with fruit and sometimes loose change. In the evenings from 9 p.m. to 3 a.m., groups of adults gather in front of the houses of newlyweds where they strike up ancient songs that augur prosperity and also request *su cocone*, this special bread in the shape of a cross.

There is a large production in Sardinia of the more finely crafted breads that require a good deal of skill. There are the breads for weddings, the breads used in religious festivals – fashioned into allegorical shapes – and above all, those in the shape of horses, handbags and dolls for children, not unlike edible toys.

The bread that is eaten on a daily basis must meet the needs of the shepherds, who even today still spend whole seasons in the mountains. *Pane carasau* or Sardinian parchment bread, as it is also known and is now exported widely, is a round and crunchy sheet of bread that keeps for a long time. It also serves as a first course. Steeped in hot water and seasoned with fresh Sardinian *pecorino* it constitutes a kind of soup, whereas when enriched with tomato *sugo* and poached eggs, it changes its name and becomes *pane frattau*.

Beyond the splendour of the Emerald Coast and the small beaches of Gallura lies another Sardinia worth taking the trouble to discover. These are regions that have not yet become tourist traps and where over period of time I have discovered something that will always remain for me one of Italy's best-kept secrets. I have spent holidays in Sardinia travelling the unpaved roads either on a Vespa, as I did in that first vacation I spent without my parents during the summer of my school-leaving exams; and likewise on my bicycle, exploring not only the entire coast of the adjacent French island of Corsica, but also most of the Maremma, the Chianti hills, Circeo and the part of Umbria between the lake of Passignano and Assisi.

The best time to go to Sardinia is in May when nature is an explosion of colours with fragrances so typical of this Mediterranean spot, but which vary from place to place. From Olbia you take the flat coastal road in a southerly direction, through areas covered by a lush pine forest, and arrive at the Gulf of Orosei. It is worth stopping here to have a swim at Pelosa, a beach right in front of the island of Piana. It feels as though you are diving into the waters of a Pacific atoll. The long stretch of incredibly white sand and the light blue colour of the tranquil waters around the shoreline contrast with the crash of the waves that break against the rocks that appear offshore, and look very much like a coral reef.

After Siniscola, the landscape changes dramatically, the reefs of pink granite giving way to a succession of plateaux and mountains interspersed by deep valleys created by water originating from the mountains of the Massif Gennargentu. When the water made contact with the calciferous rocks it created deep grottoes and rivers that would flow underground for some kilometres before emerging. Around Oliena, 20km inland from Dorgali, the Su Golgone spring

is the most spectacular example of this phenomenon: the water with a capacity of 300 litres per
second flows over jutting rocks and comes to rest in
the River Cedrino down below.

Bandits who lived in the dark caves and
caverns once used the rambling paths, often
marked by deep and dangerous crevices and for
the most part used only by shepherds. This area
is known as the Barbagia, a region that has
never really been conquered, where you will
come across villages that are still completely
isolated from the rest of the island, and
where it is easy to discover one of the traits
which characterise the inhabitants of Sardinia: their resistance to
the influence of foreign cultures. From seams in these mountains
comes the granite which is mined in great quantities and used all
over the world. The base of the Statue of Liberty, Brisbane's
Riverside Centre skyscraper, the 15th century colonnade of the
Duomo of Pisa and the Pantheon's columns in Rome are all made
out of Sardinian granite.

But Supramonte also has a spectacular coast. Dorgali is one of
its important centres and is also the village that Gianni and
Lucia, the new caretakers of the Villa at Dagnente, came from. It
took only a warning phone call that I was about to arrive for a chain
reaction of invitations to begin. In the three days I spent in Cala
Gonone, a seaside village 7km away from the outskirts of Dorgali
and reached by a steep winding road, I was able to experience the
ancient hospitality of the Sardinians that is still considered today as
verging on sacred. Lucia had given her sister Angela advance notice
about my passion for searching out traditional recipes and local
products, which gave birth to an unprecedented and intense journey
of discovery into the local gastronomic culture. Each time I prepare
aranzada, a soft *torrone* full of orange peel, almonds and honey, the
fragrance which fills the house reminds me of the warm and

generous hospitality I received from those people – at the same time as attracting all the bees in the neighbourhood!

ARANZADA

150g orange rind (only the orange part – or buy 2 packets of citrus peel)
150g raw honey
150g coarsely chopped almonds

Put orange rinds in a glass terrine, cover them with water and let them steep for 2 days. Change the water every now and then until they lose their bitterness, then drain them. Blanch them in boiling water for several minutes, drain, and let them toast in the oven at 160–170°C for about 10 minutes. Slice them into julienne strips.

Put honey and orange rinds in a casserole on a low flame and cook them for 15 minutes, then add almonds. Amalgamate well and cook for a further 10–15 minutes or until the mixture is dense and dry.

Lay this mixture on a marble slab and let it cool before slicing it. This *torrone* will keep for weeks.

Cala Gonone is the embarkation point for visiting the beaches of Cala Luna, considered one of the most beautiful beaches in the whole of the Mediterranean, and Cala Sisine, as well as the Grotto of the Sea-ox, so named because it is home to the monk seal (*Monachusa albiventer*), of which there are only a few specimens left.

These beaches are accessible only by sea and are encircled by white limestone mountains. Oleander and rosemary bushes and mighty wild olive trees (*Olea Europea*) grow on these shores. Completing the beauty and accentuating the magical atmosphere of the place is the sound of the water that issues forth from the deep grottoes and the perfume of the particular variety of juniper that grows by the water's edge.

The southern part of the island bordered by the city of Cagliari, the capital of Sardinia, and Oristano on the west side, is mountainous and full of lead, zinc, silver and carbon mines, whose extraction has represented the principal economic resource of the area known as Sulcis-Iglesiente.

On the stretch of coast every metre of which I covered on my bicycle, I remember the Costa del Sud or south coast as being framed by a pine forest of extremely tall trees resembling soldiers on picket duty, which led right up to the spectacular beach of Chia, dominated by a 17th century tower, with a well-known golf club and numerous horse-trekking establishments. At that time it was still a wild place, composed of sand dunes and unpaved roads that led to tiny bays sheltered from the ever-present wind.

At the end of the south coast, the road rose gently, leading away from the coast. The pines gave way to cork trees with their peeling bark, looking as if they were liberating themselves from clothes. On the rocks below you could just make out the white villas that were so well camouflaged by the surrounding landscape. I hope that successive tourist developments have not disturbed the harmony between man and nature that was so much a part of this coast at that time.

But it is the island of San Pietro that holds the greatest surprises: you feel as if you have stepped into another world. The inhabitants speak in Ligurian dialect, are devoted fishermen and have a conspicuously open and jovial personality that immediately identifies them as not being Sardinians. There is a historical explanation for this. At the beginning of the 18th century the island was granted to the Ligurian inhabitants of Tabarka, a small Tunisian island where they had gone in order to fish for coral in the retinue of a rich Genovese family. Oppressed by the local authorities they asked for and were granted permission by King Carlo the Third to settle on the small, uninhabited island. In their gratitude they named this small settlement Carloforte, in honour of the king. Even the houses and the small palaces of the last century recall

Ligurian architecture, as do the local traditions and customs that have survived for centuries.

Beyond Carloforte, the lush island is a continual succession of bays that can only be reached by sea, and isolated crags jutting from the sea that are volcanic in origin. The vegetation is full of rare botanic species like the Aleppo[2] pine, the dwarf palm and wild orchid and with rare animals, among which features Eleonora's falcon, the symbol of the island.

The influences of the various migrations to the island have left their mark on a local cuisine that is both creative and unique. Alongside the *casca'* which has its origins in the North African *couscous*, a dish of refined semolina served with vegetables, you also find *pilau*, which comprises unrefined semolina seasoned with a sauce made from lobster, shrimp and prawn.

The local wine, Carignano del Sulcis, has an intense aroma of jasmine, plum and redcurrants.

In the memories that I relive thanks to the flavours of the recipes that I have collected, the thing I remember most about the island is the lamb with wild fennel and the red myrtle liqueur which is found all over Sardinia. Unlike the white myrtle liqueur common in Corsica, extracted from an infusion of the myrtle flowers, the red myrtle liqueur comes from a skilful infusion of the plant's berries that have been handpicked. Even though I really do prefer the Corsican myrtle liqueur, the stronger Sardinian version which sticks to the roof of your mouth and overwhelms your taste-buds transports me back to Carloforte's

---

2 Aleppo is a Syrian city on the border with Turkey.

small *piazza* one mild April evening. The live music, a constant feature during the summer months and festivals, is joyous in a way that invites participation, with its notes reminiscent of Arabic melodies intertwined with popular Sardinian rhythms. Paolo, his mother Virginia, Giulia, not quite one year old and I, spent the Easter holidays in Sardinia in order to discover the island's landscape and its food, and in keeping with local custom we tried *pardelus*, cakes made out of fresh ricotta, saffron and orange flower essence. We had already decided to leave Italy and I wondered how long it would be before I would return to Sardinia, without realising that I would take away with me, along with a supply of myrtle liqueur, memories that I would be able to revisit whenever I wished.

Every time I returned from Sardinia, I always had the feeling that something had escaped me. Only on reading a passage from D. H. Lawrence's *Sea and Sardinia* (1921) was I was able to put a finger on my unease. Lawrence describes Sardinia as an island without history – one whose landscape and people are like no other. It is as if the island has always existed outside of the process of civilisation – history confirms for us that Sardinia has never been completely subject to any people or power.

The explanation for this proud and indomitable place is perhaps best gained by examining the *nuraghe*, those tower dwellings in ruins that appear on all the Sardinian postcards. In the deserted countryside on the inner reaches of the island you will find more than 7000 of these structures that have been there for almost forty centuries.

Their name appears to come from an ancient word that means 'pile', and they are all that remains of a civilisation that prospered for around 1500 years, and whose advanced technology is attested to by their construction techniques, similar to those used by the Egyptians to build the pyramids. The largest complex of *nuraghe* is known as Su Nuraxi, at Barumini near Cagliari, and is composed

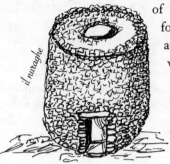

il nuraghe

of *nuraghe* huts built around a fortress that was invulnerable to attacks from battering rams. The walls of the *nuraghe* are built with heavy boulders cut to shape and held together without the use of cement or other binding agents.

Unfortunately the only testimony to this ancient civilisation are the few stones left of these mysterious *nuraghe*. But in the numerous festivals still held on the island it is easy to glimpse the pagan rituals that have possibly derived from Sardinia's ancient history. Perhaps for the very reason that we know so little about it, it manages to work its enchanting magic upon us.

GLOSSARY:

FIORE SARDO (feeo-reh sahr-do) literally means flower from Sardinia. It can be manufactured industrially with a mixture of pasteurised, or occasionally raw, ewe's and cow's milk but traditionally this cheese is made exclusively from freshly drawn, raw ewe's milk. Native Sardinian sheep are believed to be descended directly from the wild mountain sheep that still inhabit the most inaccessible parts of the island and the origins of this cheese go a long way back in time, possibly even to the Bronze Age *nuraghe* period. Production is authorised throughout the whole region of Sardinia but traditionally Fiore Sardo is made by mountain shepherds in the huts known as *pinnette*, whose central open fires give the authentic version its characteristically smoky overtones. Today, Sardinian shepherds still make the cheese in the time-honoured fashion. Milk from one milking is poured untreated into a cheese vat – once, a wooden tub was used and the vat is the only concession to modern technology – and coagulated with a paste of kid's or lamb's rennet. The soft curd is broken with a curd knife called a *chiova*, left to drain, and then cut with a *sa sega casu*, or cheese saw. The now firm curd is shaped in moulds, officially described as 'two truncated cones joined at their wider base', whose diameter is inferior to the diameter of the cheese in the centre. The moulds are immersed in hot water, so that the outer rind thickens, and then salted in a brine bath. After salting, Fiore Sardo is left to age, first in the *pinetta* where it was made on a rush trellis suspended over the fireplace, then on a platform under the roof of the dairy, and finally in underground cellars where the cheeses are periodically turned over and greased with olive oil, which may be mixed with sheep fat. The ageing process lasts for a total of two to eight months.

STRUTTO is the same as English 'lard', and was used extensively in the past for deep-frying to give a crisp result.

TORRONE is a typical Italian Christmas sweet, a bit like nougat, made with honey and egg whites that have been beaten to stiff peaks, almonds, hazelnuts and vanilla. Other sweets made mainly of honey that have a sticky consistency are often mistakenly called *torrone*.

CHAPTER TEN

Life on my own

My mother had decided to move to Dagnente, where she spent the majority of her time after my father died. It seemed like the best option since she had always loved to take long walks in the woods and busy herself with the orchard and

cape gooseberries

vegetable garden. It was also about the time that her passion for flower arranging began. Her displays became increasingly spectacular, though there were some seasonal constants. At the end of summer, cape gooseberries would form the base of compositions that would last right through to the following spring. Their tiny straw-coloured lanterns enclose an edible berry which when ripe has a delicious bittersweet taste making them perfect for coating with dark chocolate. In autumn she would use butcher's broom with its pointy leaves and bright red berries, making it perfectly suited for Christmas decorations.

Giudi went with my mother. She had finished intermediate school and was about to start secondary school so she was going to have to make new friends anyway. I chose instead to stay in Milan during the week and spend the weekends at the lake with my mother and Giudi. I had gone to live in what had been for years *nonna* Tina's house in Via Baldissera, on the same floor as *zia* Luciana, and not far from the old house on Viale Tunisia.

I shared the apartment with Roberta, who was the same age as me, and her older brother Roberto who was at law school in Milan. We hadn't known each other long but we soon became firm friends and it was the only case I have ever come across of siblings with the same name. Their parents were originally from Grossetto in Tuscany. Their mother, Vania, was an elegant woman with a wonderful sense of humour, and Gaetano, their father, was a kind and affectionate man. Gaetano, Tano to his family, was the Commander in Chief of the Air Force and had recently been transferred to Florence, while Roberta and Roberto wanted to keep studying in Milan. For part of the summer I was their guest in Florence in a house near the military base inside the beautiful park of the Cascine, where we got up to all sorts of youthful hijinks. Guilty as charged: of distracting part of the squadron of cadets on parade, engrossed in observing Roberta and I, both having just got our licences, trying in vain to take off at full speed – in reverse. Guilty as charged: of interrupting the flag lowering by disturbing with our shouts of terror the soldiers who perform the ritual raising and lowering each day. On that occasion we had been walking in

butcher's broom

the park around the lake's edge and had imprudently annoyed a black swan that on exiting the water had begun to chase us. It was only the next day that we noticed a sign with the warning 'Be careful of the aggressive swans'.

Roberta's mother thought the best thing to do was to send us back to Milan as soon as possible, into Roberto's care.

After having been involved in so many scrapes together, of course it seemed completely natural to us that we should live together and we did so for three years during which time I was able to fine-tune the recipes of authentic Tuscan cuisine.

It hadn't been easy for me to decide which university course to pursue. This issue had been discussed at length with my father and I was sure that I did not want to continue studying the humanities or 'dead' languages such as Latin and Greek, but wanted instead to learn about more technical subjects. I had always been interested in terrestrial phenomena and the Geology courses looked interesting. My father had also gathered information on a Masters degree in the United States and the idea of undertaking part of my studies overseas really appealed to me.

As a child I used to love to accompany my father to the construction sites his company was working on. Wearing my hard hat, I would listen with rapt attention to the land survey reports of the geologist that I didn't understand but which fascinated me nevertheless. All the successive building plans were dependent on the geological analysis contained in these reports and so in my eyes this was important work indeed.

Over the years I have discovered that studying the earth is indispensable to producing the best wines and for growing good crops and this made it seem even more interesting to me. In my dreams, my career as a geologist would have ranged from drilling for oil in Alaska to mining diamonds in South Africa and providing a consultancy service on which soils were the best adapted to growing tropical fruit. It was wonderful to let my imagination run wild, but without my father's guidance the choice of course was made even more difficult – I really needed to enrol in a faculty that would enable me to find a job. In the end I chose Commerce and Economics, without really knowing where they would lead and without realising that this choice would at the same time allow me to develop my true interest in gastronomy and food history.

I simply can't remember in any detail the colours and smells associated with Bocconi University, where I spent the better part of my winter days for more than five years. But I can recall with ease the smell of the freshly painted white walls of that narrow passage where more than a hundred of us students were crowded in front of the closed doors of one or another unknown lecture theatre. The harsh neon lights made our faces look tired and washed out, and the apprehension felt facing the entrance exam that we knew would decide our future inhibited my desire to make new friends. But in contrast to this gloomy memory I can also remember the deep red colour of a rose that two cheeky boys had presented to the two cutest girls in the group. I watched them as without a trace of self-consciousness they made their offering of the long-stemmed rose packaged in clear cellophane and secured at the bottom of the stem with tinfoil, as flowers are uniformly presented in Italy. Who knows why I felt embarrassed for them? And yet, the two girls maintained a cool and casual manner. They were very much alike, possibly even sisters, both with long hair, one blonde and a little taller, the other a brunette. They were dressed in the latest fashion of winter 1983: boots with a low heel, the blonde was wearing a knee-length skirt, the brunette in stove-pipe pants. There must have been a leather jacket there some-where, but I can't remember for sure. I looked them in the eye and their expression was one of self-satisfaction, rather then being touched by the gesture. It was at that moment that I knew they would definitely pass the entrance exam.

I never felt at home in that building, constantly being added to

The oldest building of the Universitá Luigi Bocconi in Milano.

over the years. The original structure had been built in the 1960s, a box with few windows that looked onto dark internal courtyards that provided little light to the large rooms with their high ceilings. The new central part of the building, the School of Business Management, was more colourful, yellow and lead grey. It had been designed by an architect who had been gifted with a certain practical skill, but with an exaggerated, rather austere style and a blind sense of duty. The Bocconi has absolutely nothing in common with the impressive architectural beauty of the old State University, once the old main hospital, referred to as the *Ca Granda*[1] by Milanesi. This was the first real hospital for the poor as desired by Francesco Sforza, the head of the Sforza family, when he was the Duke of Milan in the middle of the 1400s.

Crossing the threshold of the three wide main entrance doors of the Bocconi your perception of reality changes; you are in an ant hill, where thousands of intellectual insects, uniform in appearance, are busy in their solitary endeavours. The entranceway is

---

1   Milanese dialect for Casa Grande, which means big house.

spacious, with several intersecting flights of stairs. The bar and the designated recreation areas are found in the basement of the building. This area is spacious too and comprises a succession of rooms constructed on different levels, with little thought given to acoustics. The excited voices of those who have just sat an exam and the subdued and nervous voices of those about to resit exams are all mixed together with the laughter of those who find themselves in neither situation and the constant noise of the espresso machine and the vapour jets of the *cappuccino* maker. The neon lights transform the colours of the *panini* so that even they seem bland. A long underground passage links the bar to the library. I tried to study there a couple of times, but was discouraged by the long waiting list of those trying to secure a study table as well as by my own constant sense of not belonging to an environment where everyone seemed to know each other.

Lunch was also an opportunity to stretch your legs in the fresh air, even if it was in the middle of the infamous Milan traffic. As a result of the hunger of an ever-increasing student body, dozens of bars had sprung up, offering a multicoloured array of *panini*.[2] The bar in Italy is the daily meeting place for every occasion. At breakfast time before school, I would frequent the Tre Marie bar in Viale Piave, with its curved counter covered with an elegant tablecloth. The sugar bowl and milk jug were placed in the centre of the counter. To one side in a container with a clear cover were the *brioches* that constitute breakfast for Italians; you would help yourself with those tiny paper napkins that are so hard to extract from their unsteady serviette dispensers – they either tear, or you end up with a whole handful. There were plain *brioches* with jam or with *crème patissière*, *croissants*, puff pastry plaits with raisins, 'Venetians' sprinkled with sugar granules. I preferred the soft *brioches* to the buttery puff pastry *croissants*. Nearly every morning

---

2 Panini doesn't refer to the type of bread used, but to two slices of bread of any type with a filling – a sandwich.

for five years I would skip breakfast at home for a wholemeal *brioche* with honey and a *latte macchiato* – hot milk with a drop of coffee in it – while I chatted with Miki to the rhythmic dull thud in the background of the coffee filter as it was emptied by being banged against the wooden container. Who knows if they used all those grounds to enrich the soil around the plants, like my grandmother used to do?

Much later I would take my coffee break with my colleagues from the office where I worked in Piazza San Babila, at the Gin Rosa, a historic Milanese bar, famous for the pink gins which gave the bar its name. These days even the owner of the Gin Rosa has capitulated to the excessive power of the fashion industry and there is a designer clothes shop where the bar once was. From 8 to 11 in the morning, the two coffee machines would be going without interruption, while the customers would stand in two lines, arriving in quick succession, barely pausing for their two sips of the black liquid. It was an assembly line that gives you a good idea of the frenetic life of the city.

During my university years I would spend the lunch break at Luciano's Bar in Viale Sabotino on the corner of Via Sarfatti. The counter is divided into two parts, one part occupied by Luciano, the other by his wife and in later years by Sara, his daughter. Luciano would begin to prepare the ingredients for the *panini* from early morning on, grilling the eggplants, *zucchini*, capsicum and onion on electric elements. On the bench behind him was the meat slicer, its metal blades making a clunking sound, used for the salamis, which were sliced only when the *panini* were prepared, and bags full of *filoni*, a long Italian version of the *baguette*. He used them for the *panini* with *bresaola*, *rucola* and Grana Padano cheese, *pane casereccio* for the ones with *scamorza* and smoked ham; *ciabattine* for my personal favourite *panini*, the ones with grilled eggplant, capsicum and zucchini, mozzarella and oregano. From the low and deep refrigerators under the bench would appear tubs full of snow-white fresh *mozzarella* submerged in milk, yellow smoked *scamorze*, with their characteristic narrowing that makes them look like funny pears with really short necks. There were whole cured hams, strung up like hanged men, with their long bone and stamped with the large red crown which identified them as being *prosciutto di Parma*, and the squat pink legs of cooked ham and the fat *mortadella* with its large white dots.

Nearby, in the Piazza of Porta Vicentina, the Bar Gattullo, famous for its selection of appetisers to accompany the evening *apéritif*, had had the clever idea of introducing the concept of the *primo in piedi*, which was a first course of pasta or risotto, cooked on the spot and consumed standing. Every day, at the exact same time, Fiorenzo would cook – depending on the availability of produce at market and his own whimsy – *pennette* with salmon or seasonal vegetables, mushroom risotto in autumn, nettle risotto in spring, and *rucola* and shrimp risotto in summer.

Then there was the more prized Prosecco[3] risotto. This is the more economical version of Champagne risotto – an ideal recipe for any bar that has a daily stock of partly consumed bottles of sparkling wine.

RISOTTO AL PROSECCO

1 litre vegetable broth
1/2 onion
80g butter
350g *carnaroli* rice
50g grated Grana Padano cheese
2 1/2 glasses sparkling *rosé* wine
freshly grated white pepper

---

3 A sparkling white wine from the Veneto region.

It is essential that the *carnaroli* variety of rice is used, as
this risotto not only needs to rest but will also have
extra wine added to it at the end of cooking. The grains
need to remain *al dente* for quite a while. The sparkling
wine shouldn't be too dry (that is, not *brut*) otherwise
acidic elements will come through. This is why a *rosé*
wine with its residual sweetness is advised.

Heat vegetable broth in a small saucepan and
keep hot.

Mince onion and braise with a knob of butter
over a low flame for 2 minutes. In a casserole
toast the rice with half the remaining butter,
moisten with ½ glass of sparkling *rosé* wine and
stir until evaporated. Use a wooden spoon when
adding the stock.

Cook for about ten minutes then add braised
onion. Season to taste and finish cooking.

Remove from the heat and gently stir in
grated cheese, white peppercorns, butter and the remaining wine.

Cover and leave to rest for at least one minute.

Sparkling wine, at times referred to incorrectly as *prosecchino*, has
been the most popular *apéritif* for Italians over the last 15 years. It
supplanted the more refined cocktails of the seventies and eighties
at a time when one of the most fashionable bars in Milan for
cocktails and snacks was the Bar Basso. This was my favourite place
when I was a child and my father would take me there whenever
possible. Gianni, the elderly waiter who always served us, would
patiently refill the little dishes of snacks that I had voraciously
emptied. The small tables covered with long pink scalloped
tablecloths were laden with potato chips, which in those days I was
only allowed on these occasions; olives from different regions –
small black *taggiasche* from the Ligurian Riviera of Ponente, red
and delicately flavoured Gaeta olives; delicious and unusually

flavoured triangular canapés of an infinite variety that can nowadays be found in photographs in cookbooks such as the Italian *Cucchiaio d'Argento*,[4] or the French *Pellaprat*. But the Bar Basso had its own speciality, mini-toasts: ham and cheese between two pieces of toasted bread. That was when cheese slices were first introduced. They were the thinnest slices of cheese melted in such as way as to resemble plastic. Most Italian mothers were reluctant to let their children eat them, making the same remarks and expressing the same suspicions that they have today on the subject of genetically modified food. The mini-toasts were served cut into three, giving them the appearance of canapés. They were simple but delicious.

Years later I can still remember my first semi-alcoholic drink: the Rossini, made of strawberry juice and *prosecco*. It was probably the first *apéritif* I ever had without my parents around and it was when I was about to sit my final exams. My father had died a few months earlier and I tried to ease the strong sense of loss I felt by frequenting the places I had gone to with him, in the company of my old school friend Simona, and Roberta and Roberto. That year we constituted a kind of atypical nuclear family. Around dinnertime, and in turns, one or another of my closest friends would appear. My passion for cooking had already become known and appreciated. And they had all been victim, willing or otherwise, to my disastrous and inedible experiments, like my hot chocolate which as it cooled became glue-like, or the many deflated soufflés and the 'Clockwork Orange' cake. They always brought a dessert or a bottle of wine and it was obvious that they intended to stay for dinner.

When I had lectures only in the morning, I would go home for lunch and from time to time would dine with my aunt. Like my father she had a sharp sense of humour and a propensity for

---

4 *Silver Spoon.*

*Me with ʒia Luciana
and nonna Tina, 1971.*

laughter that was contagious. Particular and thorough as far as
housework and order was concerned – she liked to refer to herself
as a 'domestic manager' rather than a housewife – she led a busy
life, dining with friends and family, going on overseas trips and
moving between her properties in Santa Margherita, Dagnente and
Madesimo.

She had always had excellent taste when it came to decorating
the houses, and the one that she had moved to in order to be closer
to her mother, *nonna* Tina, had a special charm all of its own, with
its antique furniture, the huge pale-coloured velvet armchairs and
an endless number of photographs of the family in silver picture
frames. I can recall one in particular that I would have loved to
have had; it was of my aunt as a girl, with a simple pale-coloured
dress and a flower in her hair. One day I asked her where she was
when the photo was taken and she told me that she had been at
a dance.

She absolutely loved dancing, ever since she was a child, when the festivals in the *piazza* at Modena were one of the few opportunities for entertainment. *Nonna* Tina would entrust her with the care of her little brother, my father, who was eleven years her junior, but she didn't mind as this also gave her an excuse to go out in the company of gallant young men without causing my grandmother any anxiety. And my father knew exactly how to take advantage of the situation, leaving my aunt alone in exchange for money that he would use for ice-cream or going to the movies.

Needless to say, her husband did not share her interest in dancing in any way, shape or form, as is often the case with married couples. But this didn't discourage her in the least. One summer she even had the floor of the porch at the villa at Dagnente waxed in order to create a dance floor. She managed to infect others, who had absolutely no interest in her passion, with the desire to dance.

Once after lunch while she was washing the dishes – including the coffeepot, with lots of soap, a real sacrilege for coffee lovers – wearing her slippers and that funny hairnet that always framed her lovely face, she showed me the steps for the cha cha. She listened and moved gracefully in time to the music, transported back in time to the dancehalls of her youth, while I was only able to witness her joy and remain immobile and silent in order to avoid bringing her too abruptly back to the present.

Among her vast repertoire of recipes, my favourites, apart from her secret *pâté* recipe, remain her classic vegetable *stracotto al barolo*, and the fresh herb risotto which I cooked so often during the summer that I was pregnant with Giulia that Paolo now has a permanent aversion to it!

STRACOTTO AL BAROLO

800g choice cut of beef, whole piece
1 onion
2 carrots
1 celery stick
1 clove garlic
1 sprig rosemary
one or two bayleaves
salt and pepper
1 bottle Barolo wine (or full-bodied red wine)

This is served as a main dish as the meat cooks in a good deal of *sugo* or sauce and disintegrates into tender pieces, which can then be used for making risotto or for adding to pasta. The choice of the cut of meat is important because the meat must be cooked for a long time, giving the recipe its name of *stracotto*.[5]

Of course *zia* Luciana would say that the right wine would determine the final result of the casserole. I recall her marinating the beef in a pot, covered by the wine and roughly chopped vegetables and herbs the night before.

The next morning she'd cook it all, covered and without browning the meat first, on a low flame for about an hour and a half, and add more wine if required.

The meat would be sliced, and the pot brownings sieved. The brownings would be returned to the pot with a knob of butter and a teaspoon of cornflour or flour to thicken the sauce. The sauce would be heated briskly for a minute then poured over the meat.

---

5   *Stra* = over, *cotto* = cooked; overcooked, cooked for a long time.

GLOSSARY:

BAROLO is a top quality red wine from Piedmonte, produced from grapes from the *nebbiolo* vine. Barolo has a high alcohol content and should be cellared for two to three years.

CHAPTER ELEVEN

Sun, sea and Vesuvius

In my own personal classification system apples symbolise health, 'an apple a day keeps the doctor away'; the strawberry is transgressive – in love stories it is combined with champagne in seductive dinners; cherries are agonised – the season lasts such a short time and when you buy them they never last very long themselves; the tomato is happy, the name *pomodoro* coming from *frutto dorato* or golden fruit, the colour of the summer sun, my favourite season; the artichoke is elegant, like my mother's evening gowns, multilayered with hidden zips and buttons; and eggplants are joyful, not because they are innately so but because they remind me of the joy for life I experience every time that I go to Naples.

Parmigiana di melanzane is the 'death' of eggplants, a rich dish that Neapolitans serve as a side dish and is sometimes mistakenly called *melanzane alla parmigiana*. At a memorable dinner with

Salvatore, a Neapolitan friend of the family,
we were faced with the umpteenth course
and had already given up counting
calories, simply fighting for survival.
His mother in replying to our protests when faced with the above-
mentioned dish made the irrefutable
statement: 'Well, what are you making such a fuss about, it's only vegetables, it can only do you good!'

The tomato sauce is made by
cutting in half 2kg of fresh tomatoes,
or 1.5kg of peeled tinned tomatoes,
putting them in a colander and letting
them drain for half an hour, then put-

melanzana

ting them on to cook with a finely diced onion and
10 leaves of basil. Cook for ten minutes then leave to cool, get rid
of the excess water and strain through a sieve. If the salsa isn't a
good thickness at this point, return it to the heat until it becomes
the right consistency (it should not be watery). Add salt to taste
at the last moment.

It is well known that depending on their freshness and on the
variety, eggplants can be bitter. There are two solutions to this
problem: either cut the eggplants into thick slices, cover them with
refined salt and leave them to absorb the salt for 20 minutes to half
an hour, rinse and then dry them; or simply try them! If they
aren't bitter at this point they won't be after they have been
cooked. The latter method may seem unsophisticated, but it saves
a great deal of time.

I use the same method for pumpkin, but while I haven't yet
managed to find a use for eggplant scraps, apart from in the
compost, pumpkin has proven itself to be an inexhaustible source
of richness. It is the strongest face-mask I have ever tried; it
softens and detoxifies the skin. Crush the left-over pumpkin pulp

and everything else, add a bit of yoghurt and you are all set to go. I don't look at myself in the mirror and I won't open the door to anyone, not even my mother, but the results are worth it.

Cucumbers are a different story. My mother has always made good use of them. When we were children at the beach, she would give us slices of cucumber when we were thirsty, unperturbed by the fact that they are difficult to digest. When she sunbathes she put slices of cucumber on her eyes to protect them. The cucumber's moisturising and soothing properties make it, along with potato, an ideal after-sun treatment. In salads she cuts it into thin slices and seasons it with salt until the excess moisture has evaporated, then adds chopped mint leaves, olive oil and salt and you have a refreshing summer salad. And it wouldn't surprise me if she used the left-overs as hand cream!

PARMIGIANA DI MELANZANE

Cut 1kg of eggplants into half-centimetre slices and fry them in boiling oil. I prefer to grill them on the barbecue or on a hot plate, but I don't tell my Neapolitan friends. Cut into strips 300g of *mozzarella* and a whole bunch of fresh basil leaves.

Put three spoonfuls of the tomato salsa into a 23cm baking pan and add a third of the eggplant, gently layering it. Then sprinkle two spoonfuls of grated Parmesan, 10 strips of basil and a third of the *mozzarella*. Do another layer exactly the same and after having covered it with the remaining eggplant finish off with another two spoonfuls of grated Parmesan, and the remaining *mozzarella* and basil. Cover the whole thing with salsa and put it in the oven at 100°C for half an hour; and just before serving pop it under the grill for two minutes until it is golden brown. The *parmigiana* should be served warm or, better still, cold.

The only prerequisite for success with this dish is the quality of the ingredients. In my version of the recipe, I don't use *mozzarella campana* (from the Campania region of which Naples is the capital) or s*ammarzano* tomatoes and this deviation from tradition made me so uncomfortable that I wrote to my good friend Enrico asking his advice. His reply, so typical of the elegant and gallant style of the Neapolitans, was as follows:

Dear Raffaela

I absolve you of the sin of preparing eggplants in this manner; the circumstances justify it, but the important thing is to repent! As they will be delicious in any case, you can tell whoever eats them that the original recipe is even better.

The face of Naples has changed, most definitely for the better, since my first visit, but its spirit has remained the same. Understanding the true nature of the Neapolitans takes time; the city can't be studied, only absorbed. To do this you have to go there, not as a tourist but to live. The heart of Naples beats in the city streets among the people, along Mergellina's waterfront, in the alleyways of Spaccanapoli and in the villas of Vomero. Naples has

a thousand faces, but it is always sincere and you either love it or hate it. When you go to Naples it is important to abandon all prejudices and be ready for a human experience that is surprisingly enriching. The city is slowly recapturing the timeless elegance of its castles, noble palaces, monasteries and cloisters of more than three thousand years of history. Art treasures buried for decades in the alleys of the poorer quarters are being rediscovered.

Naples is characterised by three things: the sun, the sea and Vesuvius. You will find their philosophy of life firmly rooted in the love/hate relationship Neapolitans have with these forces of nature.

The year after I graduated I worked for the university and was sent *in missione* (as assignments that took place off-campus were called) to study the management reorganisation of one of the city hospital complexes, which included the whole health system dating back to the Bourbon period.[1] Naples airport is not known for its modernity, efficiency or good organisation, with neon lights that often don't work, departure lounges that stink of smoke and the ever-present air of uncertainty that surrounds flight departures. We landed only an hour late which, all things considered, is good going. The driver who had come to collect me held a piece of paper with my name scrawled on it; he was tanned and wore a soccer shirt, with an easygoing but clearly amazed expression. He told me as soon as we got into the car that he was expecting a completely different *Dottoressa*.[2] '*Dottoré*,[3] I don't mean to be rude,' he says, 'I was expecting an older woman.'

---

1 The Bourbons were the royal family of French origin who along with the Hapsburgs, were the most powerful princely family in Europe. The Bourbons ruled Naples from 1731 to 1860.

2 In Italy laureates in all disciplines are given the title of *Dottore*, or *Dottoressa*. It is a reference to social/educational status rather than referring to the medical profession.

3 Neapolitan habit of shortening words: *Dottoressa* becomes *Dottoré*.

On the short drive to the Nuovo Pellegrini hospital, where the Professor in charge of the project is waiting for me, I reflect on these words that I am not sure exactly how to interpret.

It is May, but at this latitude it's already quite hot. The thing that strikes me the most is the colour of the sea, electric blue. The sun isn't blinding like it is in Sicily, quite the contrary. Here it makes the outlines of the palaces and people more distinct and the colours more intense. If the sun has to fight the smog and fog to be seen in the north, and in the deep south it blazes mercilessly, in Naples it seems to harmonise beautifully with the other elements.

A pleasant sensation comes over me, a memory of many years earlier when the *Endless* was still moored at the jetty of Santa Lucia, right under the yellow Castel dell'Ovo – literally the Castle of the Egg – which rises up over a cliff of tufa a few metres away from the Riva di Chiaia waterfront. As legend would have it, this is the cliff where Partenopea, one of the mermaids, committed suicide because of Ulysses' indifference to her song.

The castle was originally built in the first century BC as a luxurious residence for the Roman commander Lucullus – a lover of fine food, and renowned as such, so much so that today the adjective 'Lucullian' is still used to extol an excellent meal. Then it became a convent, then a prison, and then a noble residence again.

Rich in history, but above all in mysteries and legends associated with it, the building's fascination lies not in the baroque restored rooms, but is instead concealed in the secret passages supported by low columns and arches that make it easy to believe in the legend which has given it its name. The poet and magus Virgil is said to have placed an egg inside a pitcher suspended in a wire cage in the building's foundations. The belief is still held today in the Neapolitan collective imagination that if the egg was broken the walls of the castle would be stormed and the city would become victim to misfortune.

Every year on 19 September, the city waits anxiously for the liquefaction of the blood of San Gennaro, the much-loved and omnipresent patron saint of the city, credited on numerous occasions with having protected Naples from the destructive force of Vesuvius. The ampoule that contains his blood is kept in the cathedral, where every year a spectacle of unusual charm is repeated which was once witnessed only by those who had been specially invited. While the dignitaries beg for good fortune from the rapid liquefaction, outside the city waits anxiously only to explode into shouts of joy as soon as the Archbishop raises the reliquary up for all to see the blood-streaked glass.

On one of my successive visits to the Professor, I discovered that he performs a role within the Order of San Gennaro, without, however, ever learning the secret of the liquefaction of the blood.

Since just the one miracle isn't enough for Neapolitans, at the same time as the liquefaction takes place in the cathedral, in the church of San Gennaro at Pozzuoli, on the very stone where the saint is said to have been decapitated, the faded stains of alleged blood are said to become a brighter red colour. As is the case with many local legends and traditions, there is never just the one truth or a scientific explanation. For Neapolitans, scientific explanations are meaningless; legends, traditions and magic are part of their character. In response to a thesis expressing uncertainty regarding the sanctification of the city's beloved patron saint, a sign appeared beneath the statue of San Gennaro. Written in colourful dialect was the rebuttal: 'San Gennaro couldn't give a toss.'

Castel dell'Ovo towers over the picturesque village of Borgo Marinari with its restaurants that have for decades been the flagships of fine cuisine in Naples: La Bersagliera, Zi' Teresa and the Transatlantico. But in those days the Borgo was mainly a small port for fishermen called Santa Lucia. Their nets with those small colourful cork buoys attached were laid out to dry on the fishing boats. The buoys would drip water as if they were hourglasses marking the passage of time until evening, when the nets were dry again and would be tossed into the sea once more. Dozens of identical wooden motorboats painted blue feature in my memories of this tiny port. It wasn't equipped for tourist boats but the traffic was worthy of an industrial port. Activity was more frenetic by night. This was because of the motorboats transporting contraband cigarettes, an activity that not only flourished but was also silently permitted, and which has now been supplanted by the drug trade, which is carried out on a much larger and more international scale.

In my bunk at night I would fall asleep rocked by the lapping of the water against the boat, a gentle lullaby, to be woken in the middle of the night by the deafening roar of the powerful motors as they all started at the same time. With a synchrony worthy of an operatic overture they slowly left the port to unleash their power in a roar that made me cover my ears. The bad weather that had prevented us from setting sail had made our presence acceptable, where earlier it had been viewed suspiciously. The harbourmaster was an elderly Neapolitan who spoke in incomprehensible dialect and took shelter from the summer heat inside a tiny observation booth where he had everything he needed to pass the day in idleness while getting paid: a little stove, his coffee-maker, the radio and an armchair. After a few days we were invited for coffee, which in Naples is a sort of initiation rite signifying the acceptance of strangers. He used a 'Napoletana', the name for this particular model of Moka coffee-maker, consisting of two cylindrical aluminium receptacles separated by a basket-like filter where you put the coffee. The water is put in the lower receptacle and when it boils you remove the coffee pot from the heat and

la Napoletana

you tip it so that the boiling water passes through the receptacle containing the coffee, into the top part with the spout.

The whole process is slower than it is with a regular Moka but the wait is worthwhile. Nothing is left to chance. The coffee must be a dark roast – in Naples they say that the roasting is perfect when the beans become the colour of a monk's tunic – and it should be finely ground at point of consumption and not before. The water takes longer to pass through the fine grounds and makes the wait a more heavily symbolic act as well as strengthening the aroma that seems to perennially waft over the city. When the coffee is finally ready, sugar is added as necessary – it's pointless to protest – and served in a *tazzuriella*, Neapolitan dialect for a *tazza* or cup. But we haven't got to the most important part of the ritual yet – because drinking coffee in haste is a crime! First you have to have a glass of water to cleanse your mouth and enable your taste-buds to better appreciate the unique taste of the coffee. If this ritual is well suited to the Neapolitan character where love is inextricably linked to the painful wait for the love-object, it's poorly suited to the innately hurried temperament of the *Milanesi*, who drink their coffee scalding hot as if it were a medicine. I have been infected by the passion of the Neapolitans – which they themselves describe with a complex word rich with many meanings, *Napoletanità* – as well as a passion for coffee made in the traditional Neapolitan manner. Every time that I make it in this way, the impatient question echoes among my friends: 'But when is the coffee going to be ready?'

The Professor in charge of the project is a man in his sixties, with a youthful air and the gallant manners characteristic of the noble and aristocratic Neapolitans.

The meeting is conducted with a high degree of professionalism and to my great surprise the Professor makes no time for small talk; he inundates me with dates and hands over material to examine. There is no air-conditioning in this hospital with its air of decay. Seated in an uncomfortable chair in the poorly lit consulting room,

I can't concentrate and I need a coffee. It seems incredible that even here no one has thought to offer me a coffee. I ask to be taken to the hotel and while the Professor agrees to this he passes over to me the full programme of work and meetings we have ahead of us. I notice immediately that the driver is scheduled to pass by the hotel to collect me the following morning at 7.30. Not even in Milan, the most efficient of all Italian cities – or at least so we *Milanesi* boast – do I start work at that hour!

The hotel has none of the genial atmosphere that permeates the city and the coffee there is even worse than the coffee you get overseas. But one redeeming feature is the view of the Gulf of Naples and Vesuvius that you get from the dining room on the top floor. Today, Naples is in fact the new *Neapolis*,[4] founded in the 4th century BC, three centuries after the arrival of the first Greek colonies which were responsible for the establishment of the earliest inhabited centre, *Paleapolis* – the old city. Naples' strategic position in the Mediterranean made it a centre for military and commercial activity. In the span of the 25 centuries of its history it has been subject to numerous foreign dominations that have left their traces on the architecture and monuments. Until the Unification of Italy in 1861, Naples was among one of the largest capitals in Europe.

Right in front of the hotel is another castle, the Castello Nuovo, better known as Maschio Angioino, which borders the large industrial port.

On a clear day, which you often find in this city, a child of the sun itself, the view is of the whole Gulf of Naples, bordered on the south by the Sorrento peninsula and, at the north, among expanses of almond trees in flower where it reaches as far as Posillipo. The much loved and respected Vesuvius creates a dark and threatening contrast against the backdrop of this sunny panorama. And in the sea you can see the islands stretched out as

---

4 *Neapolis* comes from the Greek: *nea* = new, *polis* = city.

if they were sunbathing under the summer sun: Ischia, the island for health enthusiasts with its highly prized thermal springs; Procida, the smallest; and finally Capri, the jewel of the Gulf.

I express my perplexity to the driver regarding the awful coffee I have just drunk and how vital it is that this aspect of local culture be safeguarded. Mauro is a handsome man with olive skin and eyes black as olives themselves. He is dressed casually, his hair is longish and he wears a flashy watch. He is courteous but has that detached and slightly arrogant manner so typical of Neapolitans before the ice has been broken. Without me asking and without him asking me, he stops at a bar that according to him makes the best coffee in the city. The coffee is great, above all because as ritual dictates it is accompanied by a *sfogliatella*, which seems perfect to me.

Back in the car, when Mauro has finally substituted *dottoressa*, which he pronounces in a singsong manner, with *signori'*, the shortened form of *signorina*, and just as respectful but more informal, he initiates me into another local art form, that of the *sfogliatella*. There are two types, the *riccia*, which is made of puff pastry and looks like a baroque curl, full of fresh *ricotta*, candied orange and lemon peel and scented with orange blossom water, and the *frolla*, which is a little bigger. The filling for the *frolla* is identical except the pastry is short pastry instead of puff pastry.

In order to underline the importance of cuisine in Naples, but also for Italy in general, you just need to remember that it was thanks to the *sfogliatella* that the Royal House of Bourbon's confectioner was conferred with its noble title by King Federico II of Spain.

The Professor is already in his office when I arrive, but when I enter he gets up, shakes my hand and leads me along the corridor of the decrepit hospital towards the bar, which I become aware of from a distance because of the noise of the coffee machine. And of course he hasn't actually asked me if I want a coffee, but by now

I am getting used to this. The morning is a succession of coffees and appointments. In the small Queen Elena Hospital, sweet coffee is served in a Moka by a cheerful nurse, who announces to the Professor that she has booked us a table for lunch as requested. Of course I haven't been consulted.

The ice is finally broken over lunch, partly because I find it impossible to talk about work and concentrate on the *mozzarella di bufala* in front of me. It is the palest pearly white colour, almost perfectly round, apart from a small pucker at its edge. When the fork makes contact with the exterior it punctures it like a balloon pierced by a needle and a liquid is released that smells of fresh milk and grass. The rubbery texture of the *mozzarella* itself is completely different. It has an unmistakable taste, slightly salty and of milk and cream. The conversation languishes because I am completely absorbed in the complex art of tasting. I snap out of it at the thought of the calorie count. And the *mozzarella* is just the beginning. Needless to say, I'm not consulted and as a consequence the meal is ordered with no input from me. Mimí alla Ferrovia is a famous restaurant in Naples, sited between the railway lines (hence the name) and the Orpheus Theatre. The Professor appears to be well known here. He tells me that he and his wife are passionate *tresette*[5] players and once a week in turns they go to someone's house in order to play. There, consistent with the genetic code shared by all Italians, the evening ends with food. And this is the restaurant where you obtain the best *mozzarella*. Partly to excuse my distraction and partly out of genuine interest, I ask what makes this *mozzarella* so good.

Mimí, a diminutive for Domenico, the son of Michele who started the restaurant in 1942, is called to help explain the origins of this world-famous dairy product.

First mention of it dates back to the second century AD, when the monks of the monastery of San Lorenzo at Capua offered

---

5 *Tresette*, literally three-six, is a game of cards, most famous in Naples.

their guests bread with a cheese called *mozza*. The name *mozzarella* refers to the way it is made. Pure buffalo milk is curdled and processed for as long as it takes to obtain a rubbery curd that at a certain point becomes *mozzata*, able to be broken between the index finger and the thumb. According to a legend the buffaloes from whom the authentic *mozzarella* derives graze at night beneath the moon and produce better milk, so the *mozzarella* that comes from them is said to come from 'a fat milk moon, bestower of subtle pleasures'. An unforgettable experience is to breakfast in the valleys around Caserta with the first *mozzarella* of the day, served on *casereccio* bread.

The *zucchini* that follow also have an incredible taste, pleasantly bitter but balanced by the subtle but persistent flavour of mint. Taking advantage of the Professor's influence here, I take a chance and ask if I can have the recipe, adding that even if in the north we can't make the authentic *mozzarella*, we do grow excellent *zucchini*!

zucchini

But as it is difficult to get Neapolitans to give away anything, even more so if they are provoked on the age-old question of north versus south – Domenico points out that one of the ingredients vital to the success of *zucchine in scapece* is *'O Sole*, as the sun is called in Neapolitan dialect, which rarely shines through the fog in Milan. I look at the Professor puffing on his perpetually lit pipe; an imperceptible smile plays about his lips that marks the beginning of a long friendship.

ZUCCHINE A SCAPECE

6 big zucchini cut into reasonably thick round slices
5 mint leaves
1 clove chopped garlic
1 glass white vinegar
extra virgin olive oil
salt

The origin of the word *scapece* is a subject of controversy; it may come from the Spanish or, according to another source, it's a derivative of *esca Apicii*, referring to Apicio, the author of a collection of recipes written in the 4th century AD. The recipe is used for more than just *zucchini*; other vegetables and small fish can be prepared in this delicious way.

The real secret is leaving the sliced *zucchini* in the sun to dry so that they absorb as little oil as possible when they are fried. They only need a few hours in the sun or else you can put them in the oven for at least a good half hour at 30°C.

Fry the *zucchini* in a generous amount of really hot extra virgin olive oil and once they have been drained, season them with the vinegar, mint and salt to taste.

After lunch and the hundredth coffee, the Professor tells me that he has taken it upon himself to book a room in another hotel because Mauro passed my complaints on to him. I am not unhappy at the thought of changing hotels, but I decide that this might be a good time to ask to have a say in decisions that concern me. The Professor explains to me that I am his guest and he must acquit himself of this responsibility to the best of his ability. It takes me a while, but I am beginning to understand the innately kind and courteous nature of many Neapolitans that has its roots in a long tradition that is so different from the mentality of the *Milanesi*. It is hard to define, but is often referred to and best summarised by the word *Napoletanità*, an unparalled virtue, and unfathomable for those who don't come from Naples. As if to excuse myself for having made an issue of it, I tell him of Mauro's kindness and of the *sfogliatella*, without realising that I am touching on a sensitive issue: where to find the best *sfogliatella*, or better still the *riccia*. And so a playful and lively challenge is issued between Mauro and the Professor that I take full advantage of, called upon as I am to sample the object in dispute.

On my return to Milan I am an expert on the subject, a little bit heavier and enriched as a result of new and joyous sensations and simple pleasures. My idea of Naples has changed for ever. I have also given my verdict on the best *sfogliatella* in Naples; it's the one at Caffé Gambrinus in Via Chiaia, which I must confess is also partly due to the incredible Belle Époque atmosphere, with its gilded stuccoes and elaborate chandeliers.

On one of my successive visits to Naples my sister, Giudi, comes with me. This time the reason for the visit is a bit special; it's not just a work trip. I have to sit the final exam of my degree to become a qualified *Dottore Commercialista* – a chartered accountant.

We book the Hotel Vesuvio, in front of the Castel Dell'Ovo, which feels like home to me by now. Thanks to an agreement with the university, because of the conference I am here to attend, they have given us a suite whose windows overlook the castle.

After a few mishaps, and lots of soap bubbles due to inexperience in using the spa bath, which Giudi had filled with water and bubble bath, we go out to dinner with some of my work colleagues, intending to calm our nerves before the following day's exam. As we walk past the Port of Mergellina I tell Giudi about the holiday we had with my father on the boat, which she can only vaguely remember. We still had not been able to set sail due to bad weather and instead walked along the waterfront looking at the spectacular contrast of Capri against the black background of the sky, pregnant

Me and my sister, Giudi.

with rain. Men shouted enticements to buy ears of corn grilled on the open fire and sold on skewers. A hydrofoil had just set sail from the port and its white form stood out against the threatening grey of the sea. We saw a flash right above the hydrofoil and then the rain arrived with great speed. Suddenly the flash took on the appearance of a vortex and you could clearly see its rotating movement – it was like a huge trumpet of water. I can remember thinking at the time that it was as if a giant had lowered a pump into the sea and was sucking the water up by means of a transparent pipe.

It's hard to estimate how far away it was, but to me it felt like it was really close to the hydrofoil. I can remember being scared, like I always am when faced with the destructive forces of nature, as when years later at Dagnente a bolt of lightning snapped the tip off the tall pine that hung over my aunt's house. My father was already quite ill and I was unable to seek the comfort of his arms that I had sought that day at the Port of Mergellina.

Continuing along the crest of the hill along Via Manzoni you can enjoy the spectacle of the two gulfs at sunset, the Sorrento coast, with Naples and its Castello dell'Ovo, and the Pozzuoli coast with Procida and Ischia stretched out in the sea, and the steelworks that are being demolished at Bagnoli. And there beneath is Posillipo (the name means 'to soothe pain' in Greek), with its pink and yellow houses on the jagged rocks that would remind you of Portofino were it not for the different stone which is used here for building.

We descend slowly to the village of Marechiaro, meaning 'clear sea', which is composed of just a few ugly houses, lots of restaurants, and a fleet of stomachs floating in a sea that is so clear that it reflects the colour of the sky and which at the time seemed to me to be the only real beauty of this place. Among all the houses that surround it, and despite being signposted by a memorial plaque, it is not easy to make out that window which has been the subject of a famous love serenade.

Quando spunta la luna a Marechiaro
pure i pesci fanno l'amore
Si rotolano nelle onde del mare
con la brezza cambiano colore

Chi dice che le stelle son lucenti
non conosce questi occhi che tu tieni in fronte
Dentro il cuore mio ne tengo l'impronta

When the moon rises over Marechiaro
Even the fish make love
They dip and dive in the sea
And change colour with the breeze

Whoever claims that the stars are bright
Has not witnessed your eyes
But an image of them is imprinted on my heart

('Marechiaro S. Di Giacomo', by F. P. Tosti)

While the Professor translates the song for us from dialect with obvious emotion, and explains it, I begin to see the place with different eyes while the last rays of the sun suffuse the tiny village with a golden glow. I realise yet again that it takes a certain skill to be able to understand the Neapolitan philosophy, according to which viewing the *finestrella* in the moonlight at Marechiaro is one of life's pleasures.

We dine on the terrace at one of the simple *trattorie*, and I can easily remember what I ate thanks to a spirited exchange between the Professor and a waiter. This is another characteristic of Neapolitans that I am starting to understand. The waiter reads us the menu of the day, which is hardly ever written down in Neapolitan *trattorie*, which are indifferent to tourists. One of the items on the menu is *gamberoni imperiali* – Empire prawns – and on hearing this, the Professor replies that we are 'in the age of the Republic'. Without batting an eyelid, as if he is simply following the script as might a consummate actor, the waiter replies, using a title clearly intending to confer respect: 'Dottò,[6] they are the only good thing that the Roman Empire has left us.' The Professor's question actually had another meaning altogether. The name *gamberoni imperiali* refers to prawns of a certain size, which are hard to get. The waiter cleverly avoided telling us what type of prawns they were. In any case I remember that they were delicious.

The day after I sat my exam I spent with Giudi, shopping and exploring the city on foot.

The old part of Naples is found behind the Hotel Vesuvio, with its hundreds of little alleyways, thousands of people, the yells and the noises that are often the only memory that hurried tourists retain of Naples.

Spaccanapoli[7] is the name of the street that divides the old city

---

6   Doctor.

7   Literally, *spaccare* = split, divide; *Napoli* = Naples. Splitting/dividing Naples.

My Neapolitan friend, Patrizia, in front of a typical bottega of Spaccanapoli.

into two parts and, by extension, that labyrinth of lanes and alleyways where you feel as if you are walking in another age. In quick succession you come across jewellery workshops, bookshops, candlemakers with their infinite variety of candles, the fried food shops with their fried *zucchini* flowers and their artichoke *frittelle*, the chiropractors and chair menders, the latter not having workshops but conducting their trade in the middle of the narrow street, which you can walk along with difficulty but where nevertheless the cars and the scooters manage to navigate at full speed. Here you also find the shops that sell horsemeat, tripe and pigs' snouts and trotters, the antique shops, the *acquafrescai* – stalls that sell chilled water *manc'a neve* (not even the snow is so cold), as the handwritten sign proclaims – and finally there are the dozens of model shops which produce the figurines of the crib and the Annunciation scene.

When I think of Naples, no particular colours stand out and the smells aren't those of plants or flowers. Nevertheless this is the Naples that remains in my heart.

We stop at the church of San Domenico Maggiore with its works by Caravaggio and Titian and where on its upper balconies the coffins contain the mortal remains of up to 40 royal or high-ranking members of the Aragon dynasty, who chose to be laid to rest in this aerial fashion rather than be buried.

Heralded from above by the two sculptural configurations of *La Richezza e L'Abbondanza*, the Galleria Umberto I is beautiful, elegant and ornate, a vivid contrast with Spaccanapoli, but once more consistent with the Neapolitan spirit which is no stranger to the eternal struggle between misery and nobility. It was built during the Belle Époque, when the world's capitals designed architectural masterpieces in iron, with floors of precious marble with geometric designs which had their central motif the *rosa dei venti*.[8] The same design, composed of multicoloured marble, reigned over the large entranceway of the wonderful house belonging to the family of the

Professor at S. Giuseppe Vesuviano, a small village at the foot of the volcano. What I remember about that summer visit is the fiery sun and the dark outline of Vesuvius which, as joyful as it made me to see it framing the Gulf of Naples, viewed from this angle also scared me. In the tiny deserted village – probably not so much deserted as having all its inhabitants taking refuge inside their houses from the heat – it felt as if I had been propelled into a different time, a sensation that made me feel uncomfortable and made all the more acute by the contrast between the splendour of that house and the wretched dwellings that surrounded it.

---

8   The *rosa dei venti* is a star with either 16 or 32 points overlaid like rose petals.

I remember the legend that has given the name to the wine that is produced here, Lacrima Christi. The Lord Jesus, observing the city from the slopes of Vesuvius, shed tears of sorrow for this place of sinners and thieves. It is said that his tears enabled a vine to sprout that has produced the famous white wine called Christ's Tears.

In the large Galleria the light filters through the dome made of glass and iron that is supported by the wings of eight angels made of copper. It is not hard to immerse oneself in the spirit of the period, when intellectuals and writers would sit at cafés, while in the evening in the Margherita Salon, the first Italian *caffé chantant* or café with singers, its two most famous stars arrive, rebaptised *sciantose* from the French *chanteuses* by the Neapolitans who have a habit of distorting foreign words for their flights of fancy. Right up until the start of the 1900s the cooks of high-ranking families were called *monsú*, a distortion of the French *monsieur*. Another distortion of the French language is a dish called *gatto' di patate*, the name being inspired by the French word for cake, *gâteau*, but it is something quite different. It is a typical home-made dish of boiled potatoes that are then mashed and made tasty by the addition of salami or ham, eggs and melted *mozzarella*, then put in the oven until the top is a golden brown.

GATTO' DI PATATE

1 1/2kg good boiling potatoes
100g Parmigiano Reggiano cheese, grated
50g Pecorino Romano, grated
3 whole eggs
1 egg yolk
100g salami (*prosciutto* or bacon)
1 bunch parsley, chopped
1/2 glass of milk
100g smoked Provolone cheese (or smoked cheddar)
200g *mozzarella*
breadcrumbs and butter for cake tin
100g butter

Boil potatoes, peel and pass through a potato ricer (a potato masher tends to flatten rather than aerate the potatoes). Add the Parmigiano and Pecorino Romano cheeses, whole eggs plus the yolk, cubed salami and chopped parsley, mixing until smooth and creamy. Finally add ½ glass of milk to the mixture.

Grease a 25cm diameter cake tin (*ruoto* in Neapolitan dialect). Sprinkle with breadcrumbs and put in a first layer of the potato mixture (half the amount). Add the cubed (or grated) Provolone and *mozzarella* cheeses, then the remaining potato mixture. Level the top with a spatula and finish with a sprinkle of breadcrumbs and a few knobs of butter.

Bake at 150°C for 40–45 minutes. Remove from oven and rest for ½ hour. Also delicious served cold. Even more delicious the next day!

The pizza, however, has a name, quality and inspiration which is one hundred per cent Neapolitan. They say that in the first half of the 18th century, out of jealousy someone played a nasty joke on a certain Totò Sapore,[9] cook to the royal court, and he was thrown in jail. The poor wretch asked the king for mercy in exchange for a dish that would have the following characteristics: it could be cooked more quickly than pasta, it would be neither a first or second course, neither fish nor meat, it would be as hot as the crater of the volcano, taste like paradise, be round like the world and red-hot like the summer sun.

The sovereign's curiosity and greed aroused, he sampled this round doughy disc, soft and crisp at the same time and fragrant with tomato sauce, and the clever Totò was granted mercy. The deficiency in this colourful legend becomes clear when you realise that the tomato was introduced in Italy only towards the end of the 18th century. A certain type of pizza without tomato was most definitely already very common among the masses at that time because it was cheap, and could be easily consumed without a plate and simply folded in four like a booklet.

In any case, the pizza had been admitted to the royal palace, to such a degree that in 1832 Federico II had a special pizza oven made in the grounds of the royal palace at Capodimonte.

The secret of the real Neapolitan pizza is in the dough, which once it is in the oven must rise not only at the edges (it is called a 'carriage wheel' pizza) but should also rise a little in the middle, in such a way that the knife sinks into the soft dough, 'like a scalpel', as the Professor explained to me. In Naples, you can easily find a pizza made in this way on every street corner.

---

9   A play on words created by popular imagination: *sapore* = taste.

The perfect risotto

Unlike most young Italian men, Paolo had lived on his own since university days. He also maintains that he cooked for himself and didn't have his meals prepared for him by a stereotypical and omnipresent Italian *Mamma*. Getting him to agree to share his 'bachelor's pad' with me had been a long and tortuous process. He finally deigned to give me a set of keys a few days after our wedding.

We lived in a new building built on one of the few empty sections of inner city land in Via Vasari, just past the arch of Porta Romana. It was a well-lit apartment on the fourth floor with the rooms set out according to their functions – so different from the houses that I had always lived in – with a terrace that looked out onto a large communal garden where a small children's playground had been set up. I arranged the main room in such a way to accommodate our propensity for entertaining, with the addition of a *fratino*, a long narrow wooden table, reminiscent of the friar's tables found in monasteries, which stood out among the rest of the ultramodern interior décor.

Weekends and holidays were dedicated to travel off the tourist track in search of the real Italy. Paolo was able to indulge his passion for photography, while I continued to pursue my study of culinary traditions and their associated cultural significance. Thanks to Paolo, who loved the practical implications of my hobby, in those years I began to discover the chefs and the cult figures of modern Italian cuisine who combined ancient flavours with creative and exciting new ideas. And at home I would put into practice the things that I had learned on my travels or studied at the Italian Cooking Institute, which promotes Italian gastronomy worldwide and also publishes the magazine *La Cucina Italiana* in Italy and the United States. Organising dinner parties for friends or the more important ones with clients was informally part of my job.

Tuesday was market day, and it took place just outside our building in Via Vasari. It was also the day dedicated to formal business dinners where I usually served fish. Sometimes I would plan a second dinner party for the Saturday when the large market in Viale Papiniano took place, famous for the great designer label bargains you could find if you were lucky and had the patience of a saint. There were the brightly coloured stalls selling fruit and vegetables – Giacomo and Lorenzo's selling early produce was always really crowded, despite the fact that there were four people in attendance to serve the customers. And then there was Tommaso's stall with produce from his own garden. An elderly Calabrese couple sold anchovies from different regions by weight, *baccalà* or dried cod, legumes and seeds, and a huge selection of olives – including my favourites, the young incredibly sweet green ones from Naples that you will find at the market only for a few weeks each year. There were sundried tomatoes which thanks to the recipe I was given by a woman from Puglia become soft and flavoursome, so much so that Paolo will concede to sharing them only with a few special friends. You rehydrate the tomatoes by boiling them for two minutes in water and white wine in equal measure. Drain them and leave them to dry on a tea towel (ideally in the sun), then put them in jars to store with either cloves of crushed garlic or oregano and capers, being sure to cover them with a good olive oil. They are ready to eat after just one week when stored like this and the oil is perfect for dressing salads or adding to pasta.

But the thing I prized above all was the incredibly fresh fish that Savinio sold whole at his stall. It took me a good year in which I had to exchange recipes and niceties in order to get him to scale and clean the fish for me. He had sea bass, gilthead and snapper as well as shrimps, prawns and langoustine – a small type of crayfish. Early in the morning before going to work I would choose what I wanted – or, to be more precise, I would let Savinio choose – and I would return to collect my purchases around 1.30 before the stalls were disassembled.

The same year that I attended the course on fish at the Cooking Institute, Guido our neighbour – a well-respected professional banker – attended *sommelier* courses. It was a perfect combination! The dinner parties we threw together remain memorable, with Guido choosing the right wine to complement the dishes I cooked.

For the *tagliolini* with scampi *bisque* and vegetable pearls he chose a Fiano di Avellino Pietracalda from the estates of San Gregorio. The sea bass fillet with herb *brunoise* was accompanied by a Ribolla Gialla de la Viarte, a wine from Friuli. The dark and milk chocolate mousse was skilfully complemented with one of the few wines that goes well with chocolate, which is usually better accompanied by *grappa* – a Recioto della Valpolicella 1997, produced by the Corte Sant'Alda Illasi in Verona, a real explosion of strong but subtle flavours.

I can't claim credit for the mousse. It comes from L'Antica Arte del Dolce, one of the most expensive *pasticcerie* in Milan. It is a perfect escape from the grey fog and winter chill, like entering Hansel and Gretel's sugar candy cottage. You enter at your own risk and exit with your wallet noticeably lighter and weighing heavier on the scales. The head pastry chef at L'Antica Arte del Dolce, Ernst Knam's creativity seems to know no bounds. German by birth but an adopted son of Milan, he is considered to be one of the finest pastry chefs in Europe. He is, like me, a reformed economist and his creed is based on a belief that beauty and goodness are found in simplicity. In dinner parties given by gourmands, there is always fierce competition to see who will bring his latest sublime creations. Every time I return to Milan, dinner with Guido and his wife, Alessandra, is an obligatory ritual that I prepare for in advance by fine-tuning the dishes to which Guido will match wines, the fruit of careful and passionate research and which come from his *enoteca* or speciality wine shop, La Botticella. The number of people who are transforming their hobbies into businesses is reaching epidemic proportions.

Looking out of the top floor windows of any of the city's *palazzos* you will catch sight of the gilded copper statue of the Mother of God, the Madonnina, as *Milanesi* affectionately call it. The Madonnina overlooks and protects the city from the top of the 108-metre spire above the Duomo, Milan's imposing cathedral dedicated to the Virgin Mary. The cathedral has no less than 136 spires and more than 3400 statues that decorate its roof. On clear days from the lookout just below you can witness the breathtaking spectacle of the Pre Alps in the background.

O mia bella Madonnina
che brilli da lontano
Tutta doro e piccolina
Tu domini Milano
Sotto a te si vive la vita
non si sta mai con le mani in mano
Cantano tutti 'lontano da Napoli si muore'
ma poi vengono qui a Milano.

Oh my beautiful Madonnina
You shine from afar
Made of gold and so tiny
You watch over Milan
And beneath you life goes on
We never remain hand in hand for long
They all sing 'it kills us to be so far from Naples'
But then all come here to Milan.

('O mia bella', by Giovanni D'Anzi)

The Madonnina dominates the city, casting a golden glow over Milan, despite being obscured by the ever-present blanket of pollution. But she is still present in the baroque palaces, in La Scala and in the hearts of the *Milanesi*. It is easy to see why *risotto alla Milanese* had to contain saffron, a golden spice with a unique flavour.

I had always believed that making risotto was an art and was surprised to discover that it is more a question of the right technique. If you learn the reasons behind each phase in the process, the mystery of how to make a good risotto will be revealed.

The choice of which rice to use is fundamental. It should only be between Arborio – probably the most commonly used at home – and the highly prized Vialone Nano and Carnaroli, which are mainly used in restaurants. The latter two have the capacity to balance absorption of the flavour of the risotto with slow starch release during the cooking process. It is, however, the Carnaroli variety that remains the choice of chefs and those cooks who are

after a perfect risotto because it is better suited to
being cooked at length, as the recipe for a risotto
requires. The saffron must be extremely pure. The
best variety is Spanish saffron which as well as
being known for its quality has a more powerful
colouring agent which creates a stronger flavour,
signalled by the risotto's intense colour. The choice of
whether to use powder or saffron threads is a personal
one. If you use threads all you need to do is dissolve
them in a little stock.

Saffron flower

There are two methods. The traditional one
requires the saffron to be added when the risotto
is nearly cooked, while the modern method
favours toasting the saffron along with the rice in
order to produce a more intensely flavoured risotto.

The original recipe calls for ox marrow, which is now often
substituted by butter, giving the dish a more consistent and refined
taste. I firmly believe that the stock is the most important element
in this recipe. A good chicken stock, with a few carrots and onion
and celery added to it, marries perfectly with this dish, which is a
real fortifier during the winter months.

To lay claim to the noble title of risotto, two phenomena must
occur. The consistency of the risotto must be both soft and
creamy, while at the same time the grains of rice must remain
whole and not stick together. It is a bit like a perfect marriage
where the couple respect each other's individuality at the same
time as experiencing the merging of their
souls! To ensure that the rice grains don't
disintegrate they have to be toasted to
harden them up for the addition of the
boiling stock.

It takes a real expert to produce the prized
creamy consistency. Stirring the risotto neither
too much nor too little keeps the grains separate

but allows the starch to be released. Even here there are similarities with marriage, particularly in the way a wife will subtly avoid attacking an issue head-on, but will instead skirt around it to eventually win the unconditional surrender of her husband.

If the making of the risotto is also an analogy for life, there is an evident contradiction. How are you supposed to soften the onion without burning it while at the same time ensuring that the rice grains are toasted? This was a question that propelled me to attend the Cooking Institute. Modern cuisine is the result of two main trends, seeking as it does to refine traditional recipes by applying the techniques of *haute cuisine*. The solution adopted by chefs renowned as masters of the kitchen, like Gualtiero Marchesi, whose restaurant was the first Italian restaurant to receive three stars in the Michelin guide, is to stew the finely sliced onion in a bit of butter and then add it just before the risotto has finished cooking. Another possibility is to simply not use onion at all, even if this will mean sacrificing the equilibrium of the dish, since the lightly cooked onion can be responsible for adding just the right balance of flavours. As we are all well aware, just as in marriage, in life too we sometimes have to resort to compromises, especially when we don't have much time for cooking. Though as far as my mother is concerned, risotto without onion is a sacrilege.

Whether you toast the rice or not, it is traditionally done in butter, but these days oil is often used by the health-conscious and then dry white wine is added. According to my mother's version of the recipe that adds the saffron when the risotto is almost cooked, the chicken broth is added a ladle at a time, ensuring that the rice has absorbed the liquid before adding more. Another vital technical aspect at this point is that the broth must be boiling hot, otherwise the grains of rice will defiberise as a result of thermal shock and the risotto will not attain the sought-after *al dente* consistency.

Should the risotto be covered or left uncovered? If you cover it you avoid losing the fragrance and you can keep the cooking temperature constant.

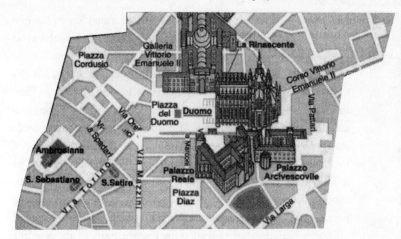

Finally, the time it takes to cook depends on the quality of the rice. The better the rice, the longer it will take to cook; add the saffron at the last minute and remove it from the heat. Now we have arrived at the crucial phase in the recipe that distinguishes a good risotto from baby food. The stirring of the cold butter into the rice, which by this time is devoid of starch, creates that creamy emulsion that unites in perfect harmony the grains of rice that have remained intact. The true risotto floats in a cream, not a broth. A good sprinkling of Parmigiano is all that is required to complete the dish.

I think that by now I have probably discouraged even the most ardent risotto fan, but if there are still a few of you left willing to meet the challenge, this is my recipe which results from many years of study, and a host of changes and refinements.

In the shadow of the cathedral's spires, beneath the Galleria Vittorio Emanuele (the longest and perhaps the most beautiful covered walkway in Europe known as *il salotto di Milano* by the *Milanesi* because of its 19th century ambience and the luxurious shops and restaurants found there), in his elegant restaurant Gualtiero Marchesi would cook a saffron risotto that was served topped with a 24-carat gold leaf. Not in the refined Savini but in a nearby locale, still in front of the Madonnina, I enjoyed the most romantic dinner I have ever had.

The lights in the Piazza del Duomo, dim but artfully placed, the façade of the cathedral with its huge door framed by *bas relief* and the stained glass windows illuminated from inside by the eternal candles, all created a romantic atmosphere in spite of the crowds that passed beneath its porticoes all night long. The shop signs of the historical locales are all the same, black with gold writing. The marble inlaid with mosaics and the statues that observe from above those who pass beneath the vaults of the Galleria all evoke a timeless age, an effect only recently marred by the many fast-food takeaway bars that have invaded the historic parts of the city in a complete lack of respect for its heritage.

I had spent a lot of time imagining this night and even more time in trying to work out what to wear. In the end I chose a skirt decorated with small coloured pearls – one of the works of art in which my mother exhibits her talents – deliberately played down by a simple red Versace top of wool and cashmere.

Paolo, fastidiously punctual as usual, was for the first time that I can remember not wearing a suit jacket and tie. He was dressed much more casually than I expected, but his style for the evening was most certainly more appropriate for the place he was taking me to dinner in his white Fiat Bambina 500. The restaurant was called La Spaghetteria – The Spaghetti House. Even now it is the place I always recommend to people who ask me for suggestions on where to eat in Milan.

I most certainly did not expect to be eating spaghetti, seated on high and uncomfortable stools while the chef dressed the most unimaginative pasta possible with whichever sauce we wanted, right in front of us. A pianist whom I hadn't even noticed up to that point graciously greeted Paolo, who leapt to his feet and left me sitting there somewhat perplexed. Paolo asked me to join him so that he could introduce me to the 'Maestro' Manusardi, whom he asked to play a repertoire of love songs.

I found it impossible to swallow even a mouthful of spaghetti and was totally unprepared for what followed. Freezing under an umbrella too small to protect us from the driving rain in the Piazza del Duomo, when we would have been much dryer if we had stayed under the porticoes, Paolo told me that one day when we were old we would remember this first evening spent together. Just along from the Galleria was La Scala, and from afar it seemed as if I could see the carriages from which the ladies descended in all their embroidered finery for opening night. It was only an illusion, no matter how well suited to the romantic spirit of the evening, but at the same time it was a foretaste of all the adventures still to come.

GLOSSARY:

PECORINO ROMANO is a cheese made from October to July using a mixture of fresh ewe's milk from the morning and evening milkings. Milk drawn straight from the sheep is filtered and heat-treated, poured into a cheese vat and inoculated with a starter culture of left-over whey. It is then heated to a temperature of 39°C and coagulated by the addition of lamb's rennet in paste. After 25–30 minutes, the soft curd is broken into rice-sized granules and recooked by heating it to a temperature of 45–48°C. Next, the curd is put in draining vats and, when all the whey has run off, is cut into lumps, transferred into moulds and pressed. This pressed curd is stamped with the DOP mark and then dry-salted several times in purpose-built rooms called *caciare*, by master salters, who are much respected professionals.

After salting, the cheeses are ready for ageing. *Pecorino* cheeses destined for the table are aged for five months while those for grating are aged for at least eight months. During the maturing process, the rounds are washed with a brine solution and sometimes wrapped in a protective film. *Pecorino* for export is carefully selected and encased in a dark plastic material that recalls the old custom of massaging the cheeses with oil and grease or ashes as they aged.

(The assistance of *Italian cheese – a guide to their discovery and appreciation*, Slow Food Editore, 1999/2000, in preparing the cheese descriptions is gratefully acknowledged.)

Ci siamo sposati

il 19 Settembre 1993

nel Monastero di San Cipriano e Santa Giustina.

Φυλή - Αθήνα
GRECIA

[signature: Paolo]　　　　*[signature: Raffaela]*

PAOLO e RAFFAELA DELMONTE
Via Giorgio Vasari 12 - MILANO

Our wedding card we sent from Greece telling everybody that we were married on 19 September 1993.

Above: Our first photo together outside a friend's old villa, 1993.

Below: Still together after nine years!

NOTES

NOTES

NOTES

NOTES